D1523567

Microsoft® Office Professional 2007 – the basics and beyond

Technology is an essential feature of 21st century life. Whether one wishes to write a letter, complete a tax return or deliver that all-important presentation at work, it is now almost unimaginable that a computer will not be switched on at some stage of these processes.

As information technology advances apace, one must be sure to keep up with new developments (or risk becoming obsolete). To help you negotiate the ever-changing world of software, Collins Dictionaries and Microsoft® have joined forces to provide you with a guide to Microsoft® Office Professional 2007.

This supplement gives you a clear insight into the basics (and beyond) of the newest version of Office Professional 2007 and its core applications with which you are already familiar.

Office Professional 2007 uses a new common interface (called Fluent) with commands and features organized around what the user wants to do, so that things are where you want them, when you need them.

This improved functionality addresses all your everyday requirements and more, whether you wish to publish to a blog using Word 2007, or guard against spam and phishing emails using Outlook 2007. Providing not only security and flexibility of use with other applications, Office Professional 2007 also includes a wide selection of Themes and Galleries to give your documents a strong visual focus and professional look.

The following sections deal with Word 2007, Excel 2007, Outlook 2007, and Powerpoint 2007 in turn. Features and functionality of the different applications are discussed alongside illustrative examples of their use.

Find out more about Microsoft® Office 2007 at

http://www.microsoft.com.

1 • Microsoft® Office Word 2007

The Fluent user interface and Ribbon in Word 2007

The main new feature of Office Word 2007 is the new Fluent interface and Ribbon. Its command tabs replace the old toolbars and menus and create an uncluttered, practical, context-sensitive way of working with Word 2007 that enables you find what you want, when you need it, more easily.

Other new features of the Word 2007 window are:

• the Office Button (used mainly to open files, create new files, publish, print and close files, and exit Word 2007)

• the Quick Access Toolbar, located by default next to the Office Button:

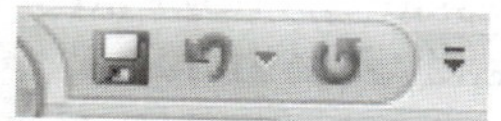

• the view controls (at the bottom of the window) enabling you to quickly see which view you are using, and to easily switch between different types of view:

• the Zoom control, enabling you to easily zoom in and out to without actually changing the document's style or the size of fonts used:

Most of Word 2007's command tabs are designed to be handy for tasks associated with typical stages in the process of creating a document. For example, the Home tab is the most useful one when typing and editing, choosing styles and fonts, copying and pasting, and picking paragraph and list formats. It is the tab that encapsulates most of what we need when doing our usual work on document.

A quick look at each of the main tabs:

• ***The Home tab*** includes commands relating to the Clipboard, font selections, paragraph settings, styles, and editing.

- ***The Insert tab*** is used to add pages, tables, illustrations, links, headers and footers, text objects, and symbols to your document.
- ***The Page Layout tab*** contains the commands for working with themes, page backgrounds, and paragraph spacing in your document. Additionally, you may choose page setup options and arrange the order of elements on your page.
- ***The References tab*** includes special elements to use when you create longer or more complete documents. On this tab, you'll find what you need to create a table of contents, footnotes, citations and bibliographies, captions, an index, and a table of authorities.
- ***The Mailings tab*** is a new addition in the Word 2007 interface. Here you can find everything you need for creating, previewing, and producing a mail merge project.
- ***The Review tab*** has all the commands you need for checking your document and sharing it with others for review. There are tools for spelling, a thesaurus, and more commands for adding comments, tracking and working with changes, comparing versions, and protecting the document.
- ***The View tab*** is where you'll find all the options for displaying your document in different ways: from basic document views, to a set of display tools for adding rulers and gridlines, to options for working with multiple documents in multiple windows.

Templates and Themes

Templates enable to you to quickly and easily produce professional-looking documents of all types including brochures, calendars, contracts, forms, invoices, memos, newsletters, and time sheets.

Using a template allows you to re-use a particular format, saving time on retyping and reformatting every time you start a new document.

To start a new document from a template, click on the Office Button and select New:

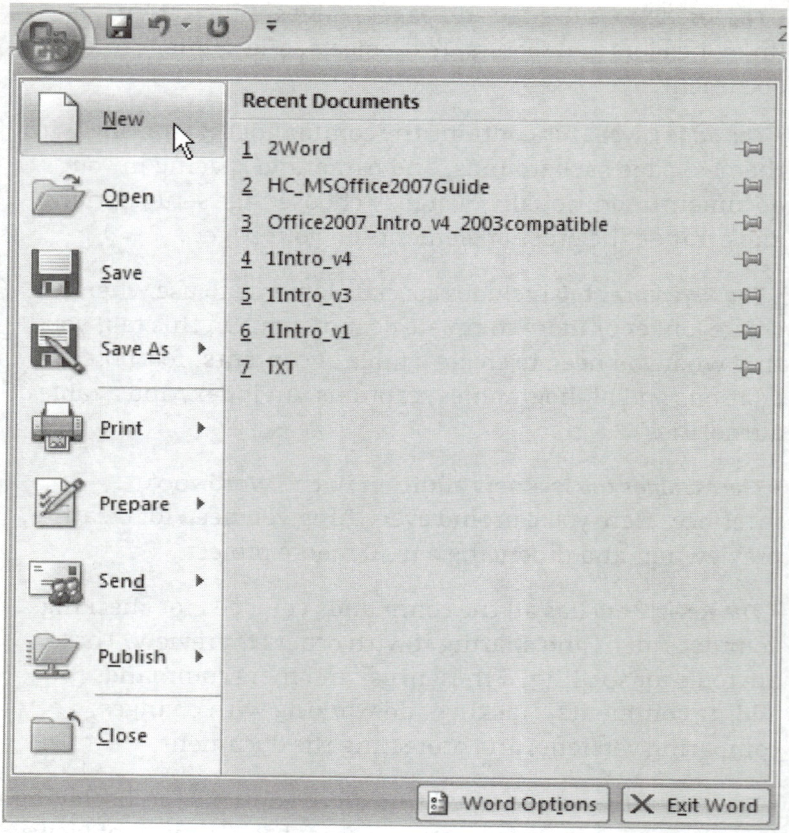

You can use your own templates (based on existing documents) or a blank template:

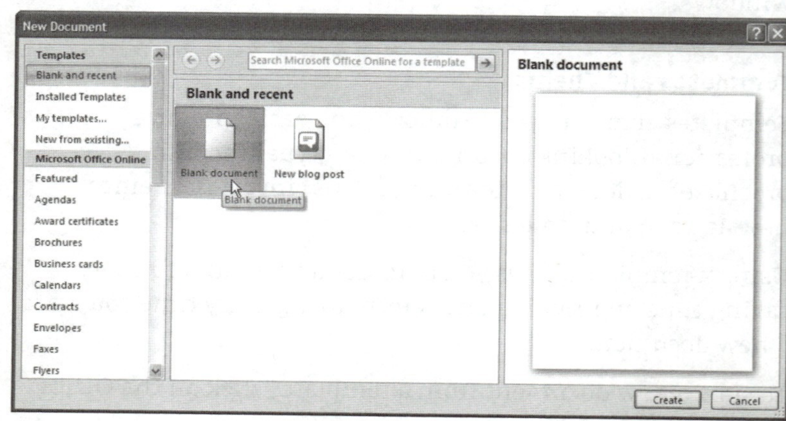

Alternatively, choose from one of the installed templates:

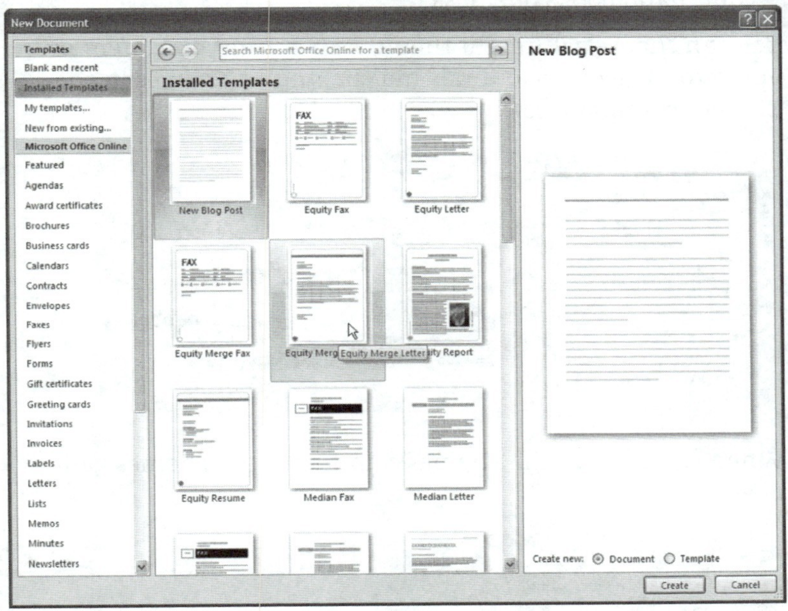

In addition you can choose from a large number online – from within the same New Document window without having to open a browser window separately.

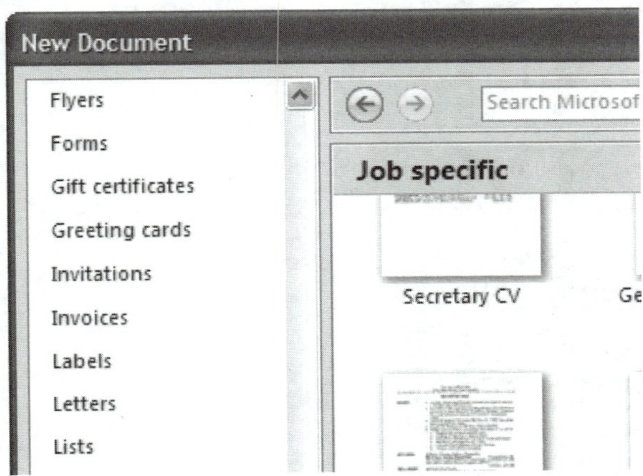

A document theme is a set of formatting choices that includes theme colours, theme fonts, and theme effects. For example, you might want to give your document a modern theme if you are designing a brochure for your IT consultancy, or an old-fashioned theme if you are designing a newsletter for your second-hand books business.

You can choose a different theme for a current document by going to the Page Layout tab and clicking on Themes in the Themes command set:

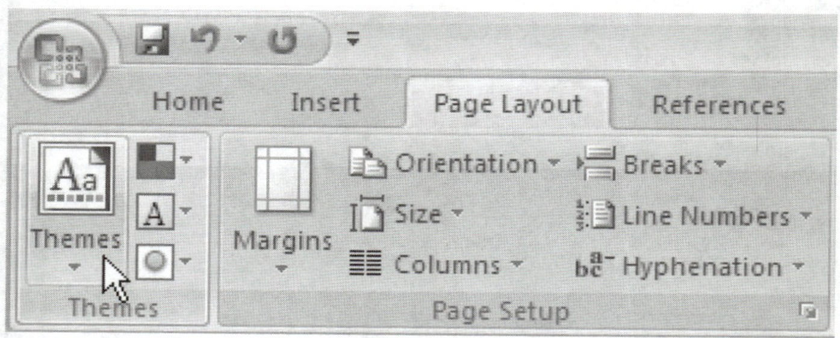

When you click on the Themes command, the Themes gallery opens:

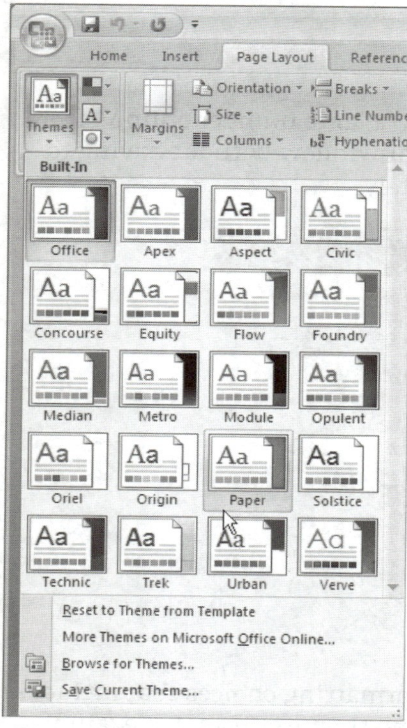

The individual theme options within the gallery show sample typefaces and colours to convey quickly the effect of each.

Cover pages

These are preset title pages with fields for title, subtitle, author, date, etc, depending on the type of cover page chosen. They are found in the Pages command set under the Insert tab in the Ribbon. The examples are picked from a gallery and follow the Document Theme.

Open the gallery by clicking on the Cover Page command. Hovering over the command with the mouse will bring up the SuperTooltip description:

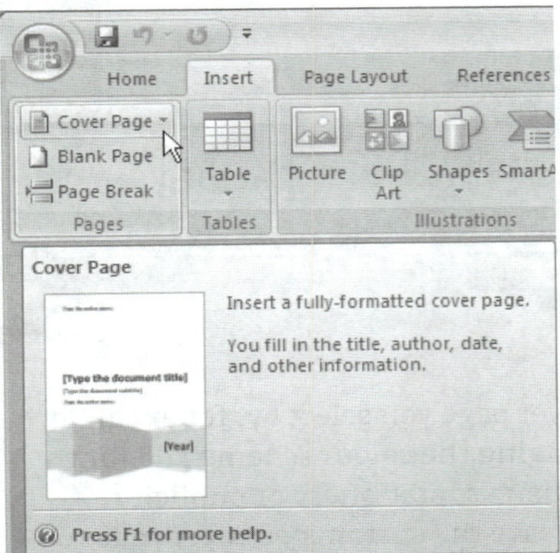

A mouse click brings up the gallery of Cover Page choices:

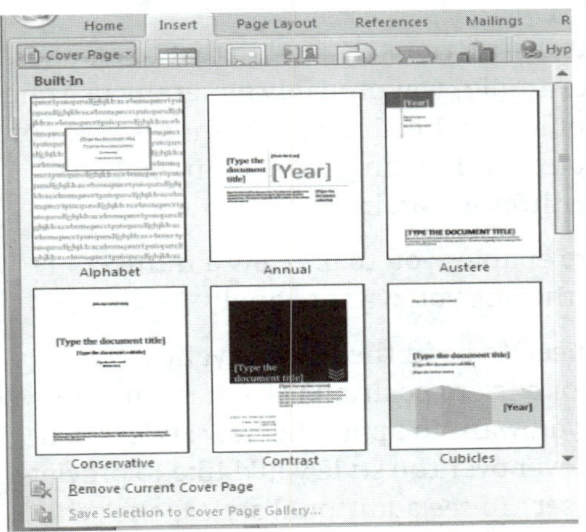

When you click on a cover page of your choice in the gallery, it is added at the beginning of your current document. You can click in the text boxes to add your own text to the page.

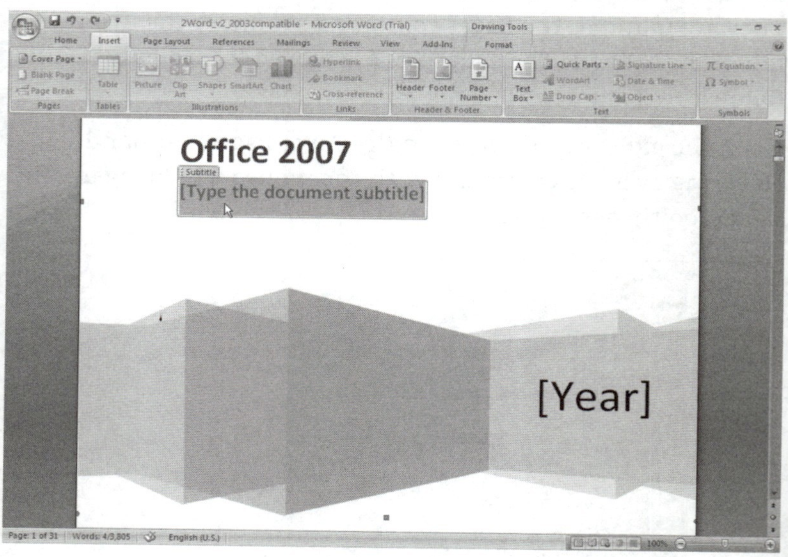

You can customize any cover page you select by, for example, adding your logo and changing the colour scheme and font style to fit your existing business stationery or publicity documents. You can then save the customized cover page to the Cover Page gallery to use it again with other documents.

Applying Quick Styles

A style is a set of format instructions applied to text to change its format details. For example, you probably generally use one font and font size for your main headings, and another font or (at least) font size for your sub-headings. The main body text will require something different again.

The Quick Styles feature enables you to preview a number of styles before you select the one you want to apply.

To preview styles, you need to be in the Print Layout view. Either select some text or click to position the cursor in your document at the point you want to apply the new style; then let the mouse pointer hover over the style you'd like to preview in the Styles command set. To see additional styles, click the More button in the lower-right corner of the style examples, and a gallery of further style options appears:

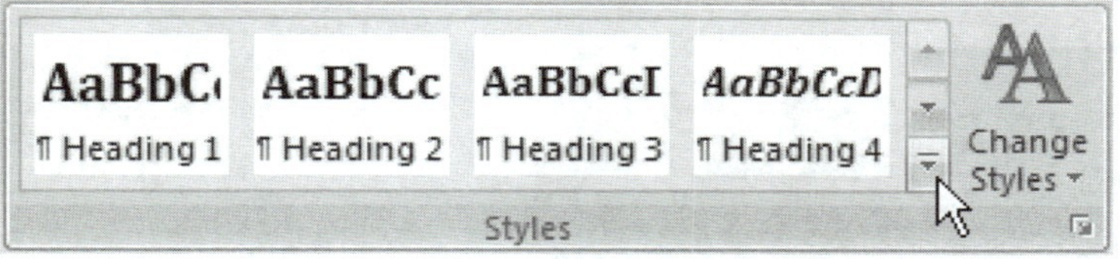

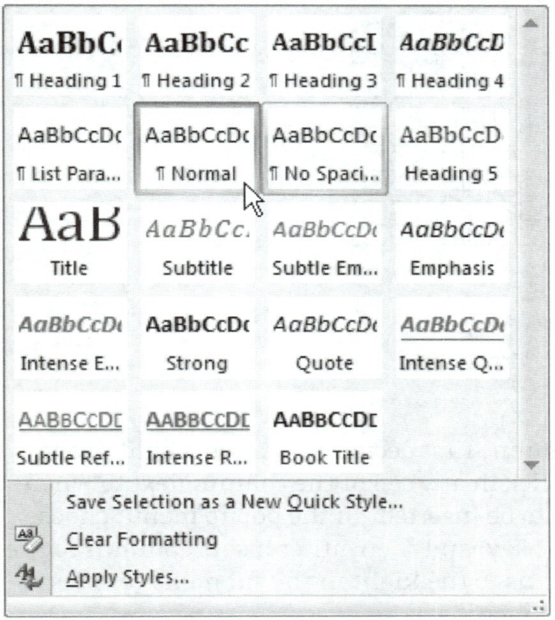

Preview a style by pointing to it in the Styles command set or gallery, and click to apply the style of your choice.

Inserting and editing tables

To insert a table, go to the Insert tab and use the Tables command set:

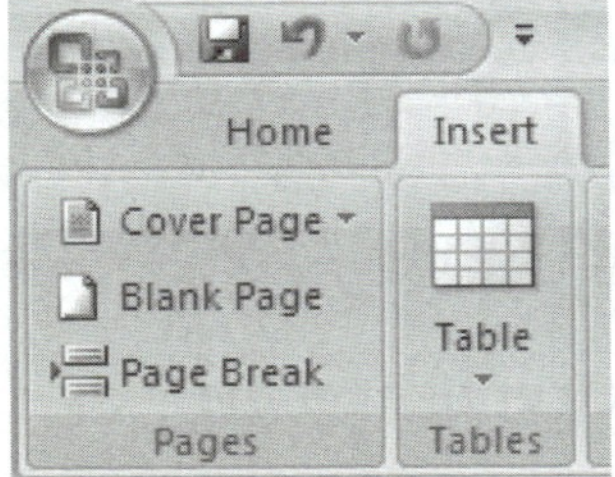

When you click on the Tables command, a dialog box opens that lets you choose the number of columns and rows for your table:

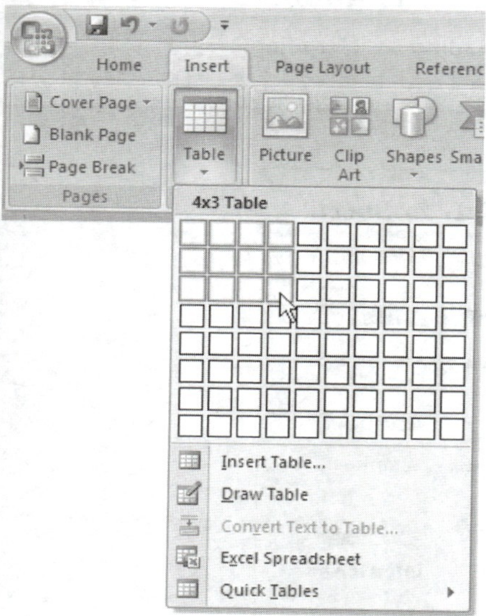

To insert a new column, first decide where you would like it to go. Then right-click in any cell of the column next to where the new column is to be inserted. In the popup menu, choose Insert (or press the I key) and then either Insert Columns to the Left or Insert Columns to the Right in the submenu (or press the L or R keys):

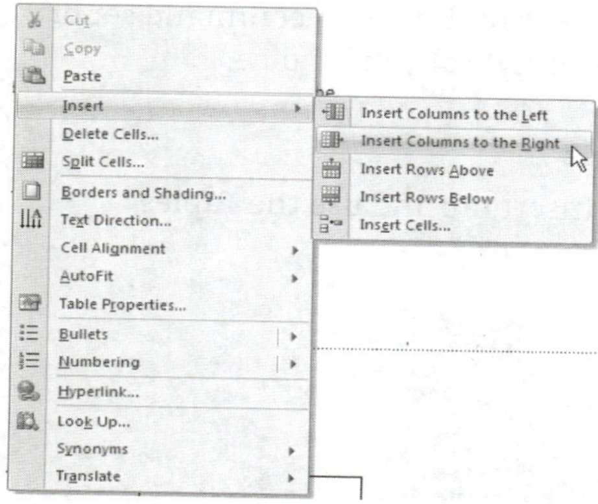

A new column is then inserted to the left or right of the column you right-clicked.

To insert multiple columns, first select a number of existing columns in the table by dragging over them with the mouse. If you want two new columns, select two existing columns, three for three, and so on. Once the desired number of columns is selected, right click and choose Insert from the popup menu, and then choose where you'd like the new columns to be inserted (left or right of the selected columns), as before.

To add rows, right click on the row next to where you'd like to add a row and select Insert again, but this time choose either Insert Rows Above or Insert Rows Below:

To delete cells, columns or rows, right click on the cell(s), column(s) or row(s) you'd like to delete and choose Delete Cells.

Make your choice In the dialog box that appears and press OK to confirm:

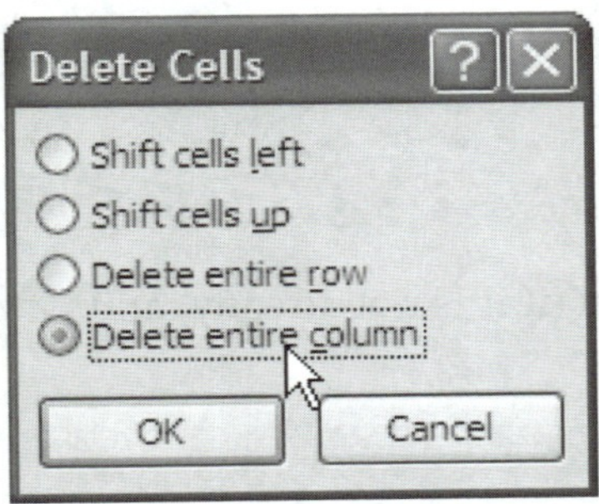

Tab Tip for Tables: When the cursor is inside a cell, the Tab key will move the cursor to the *next* cell if it is empty, or select the contents of the next cell if it is not empty. Similarly, Shift+Tab will move the cursor to the *previous* cell or select its contents. If the cursor is in the last cell of the last row, pressing Tab will insert a new row at the bottom of the table and move the cursor there, ready to start typing or pasting.

SmartArt graphics

SmartArt graphics are preformatted graphic elements (Venn diagrams, flow charts, etc) that size text to fit within them and change font, colour, etc to match changes in Document Theme.

Choose SmartArt from the Insert tab to start the process; then select one of the four basic layout styles (Process, Hierarchy,

Cycle, and Relationship) to find the diagram type that is right for your document. Each diagram style offers several style possibilities.

SmartArt graphics enable you to create sophisticated diagrams quickly by customizing them with pictures and descriptive text.

Collaborating on files and comparing documents

Reviewing is an important stage in producing documents of many kinds. The information here applies to Microsoft® Office Excel 2007 Worksheets and Microsoft® Office PowerPoint 2007 presentations as well as to Word documents.

Adding comments

When working with others on a document, you may sometimes want to add comments. To make a comment, use the Review Tab and click on New Comment:

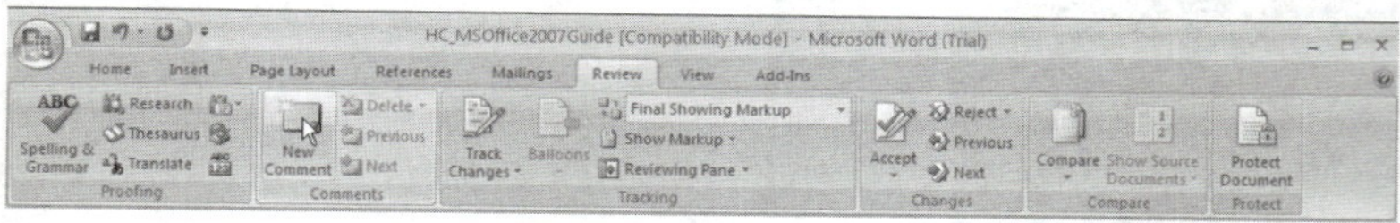

The Reviewing Pane will then open (if it is not already) and you can start typing your comment:

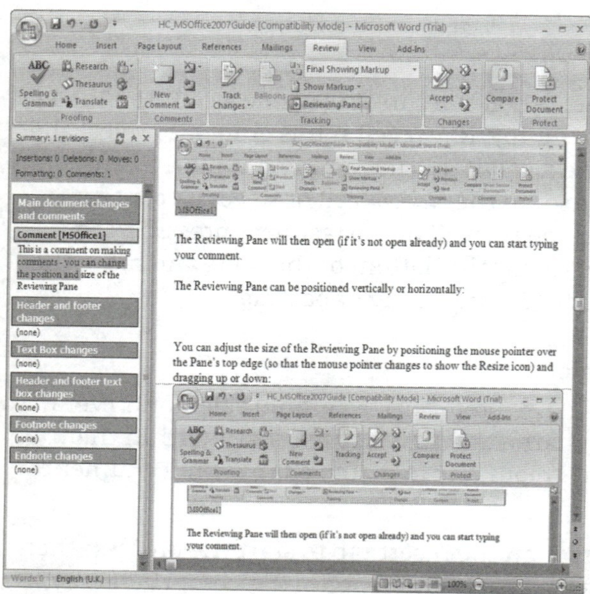

The Reviewing Pane can be positioned vertically or horizontally:

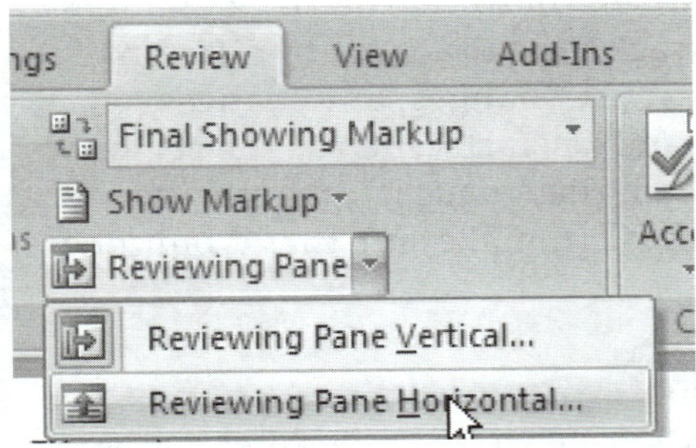

You can adjust the size of the Reviewing Pane by positioning the mouse pointer over the Pane's top edge when horizontal, or right edge when vertical (so that the mouse pointer changes to show the Resize icon) and dragging up and down (or left and right):

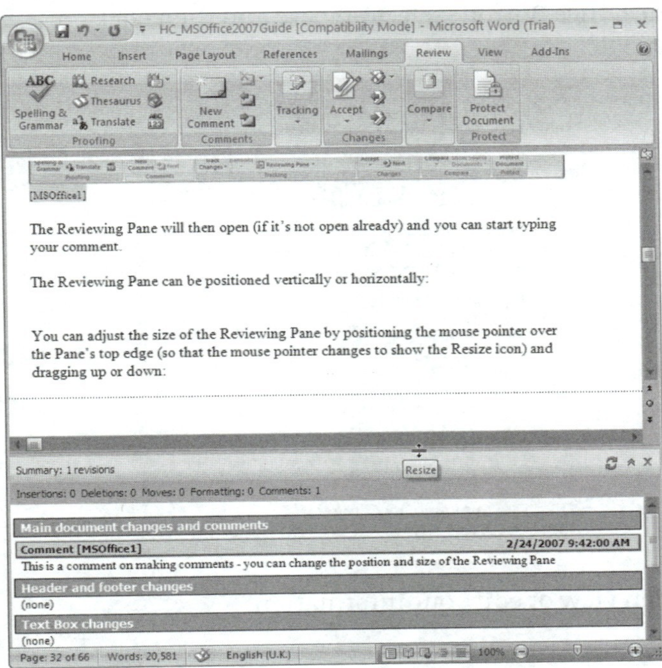

To close the Pane, click on the cross in its top-right corner. To open it again, click on Reviewing Pane in the Tracking command set under the Review tab.

Track Changes

There are times you will want to track the changes made to a document used only by yourself, however the Track Changes facility is usually used to track the edits made by different people. When you turn on Track Changes, any changes you make are highlighted and key facts (such as the person making the change and when they made it) are recorded. Before you turn track changes on, make sure that Word 2007 knows who you are:

Telling Word 2007 who you are

When you first install it, Microsoft® Office Professional 2007 will attempt to determine your identity from information already on your computer or from a previous installation. If you share a computer with someone else, install on a brand new machine, or have inherited a computer from someone else, this information may need to be changed so that it's accurate. To inspect the information Word 2007 already has, click on the Office Button, select Prepare and then click on Properties.

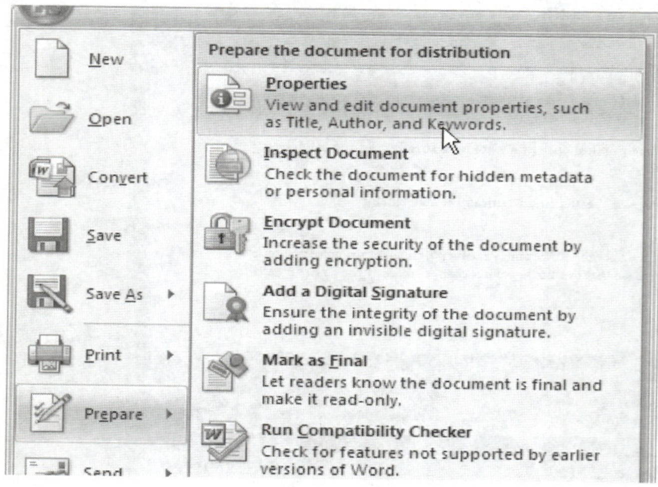

You can then view or edit your information:

Document Properties ▾ Location: E:\essentials\HC_MSOffice2007Guide.doc * Req
Author: Anne Onymous
Title: MS Office 2007 Guide
Subject: Office 2007
Keywords:
Title: The title of the document
Category:
Status: draft
Comments:

When you have finished, close the window.

Before creating new comments or implementing Track Changes, you can check that Word 2007 knows who you are by clicking on Track Changes (or pressing Ctrl+Shift+E) and selecting Change User Name (or pressing U):

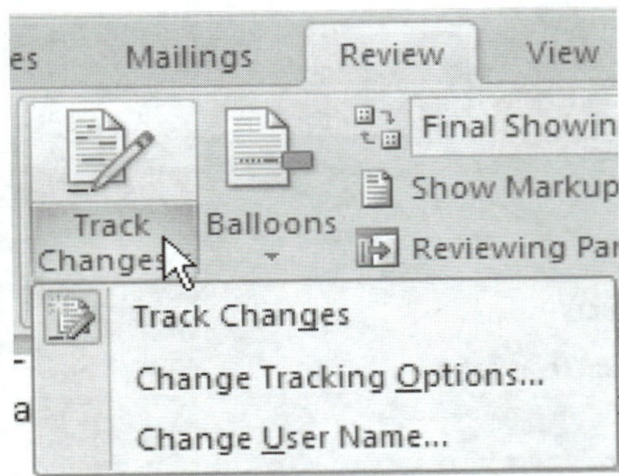

This opens the Word 2007 Options dialog box which is also useful for:

- switching between users when both working on the same document and using the same computer
- setting other popular options, such as suspending/activating the Quick Format toolbar, or the Developer's tab, etc, or some of the many other options accessible via the Word 2007 Options dialog box:

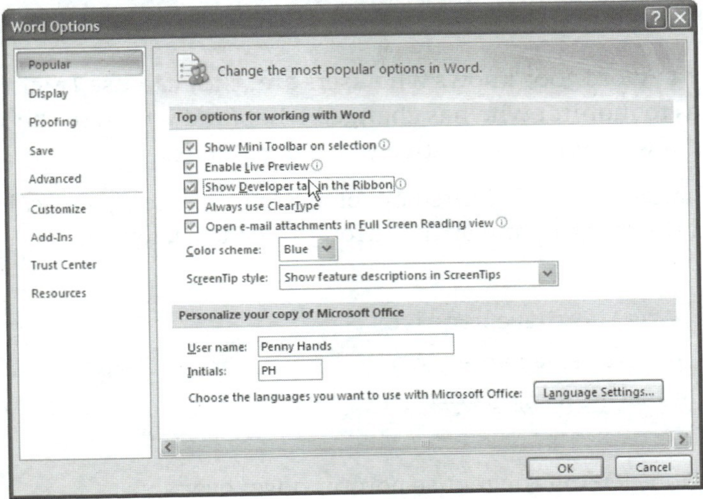

You can also open the Word 2007 Options dialog box by clicking on the Office Button, then clicking on the Word 2007 Options button (or press I while the Office menu is open):

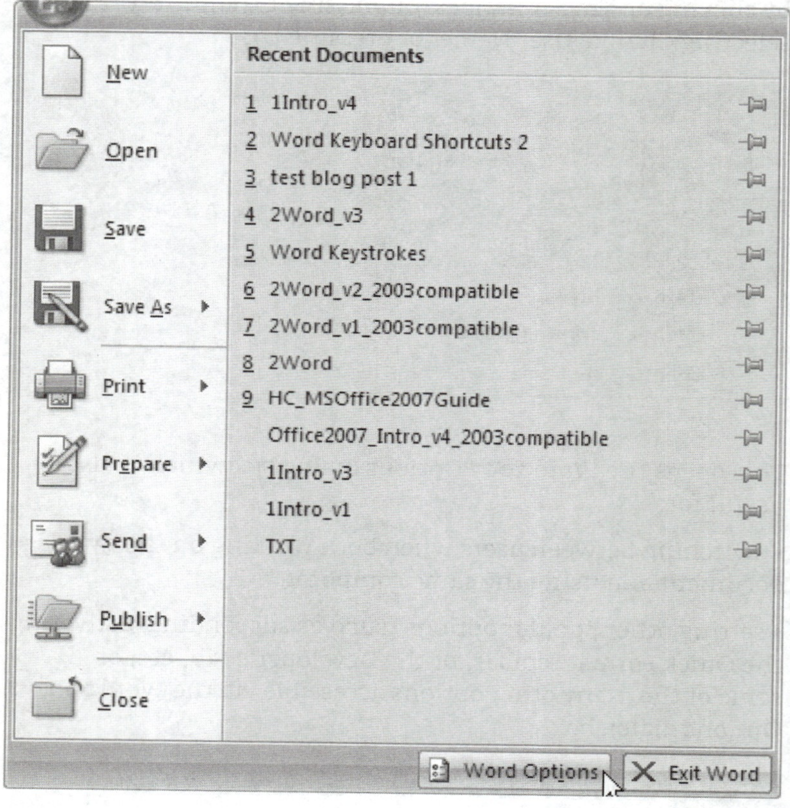

As long as Word 2007 knows who users are, they can use Track Changes to monitor who has changed what (and when) in the process of working collaboratively on a document.

Such changes are highlighted by colour-coding of text, vertical lines in the margin, and strike-through text for deletions:

When you have been wc
different file names, Wo
~~to say how to do this.~~

In addition, letting the mouse pointer hover over a

highlighted change will show you a SuperTooltip with details:

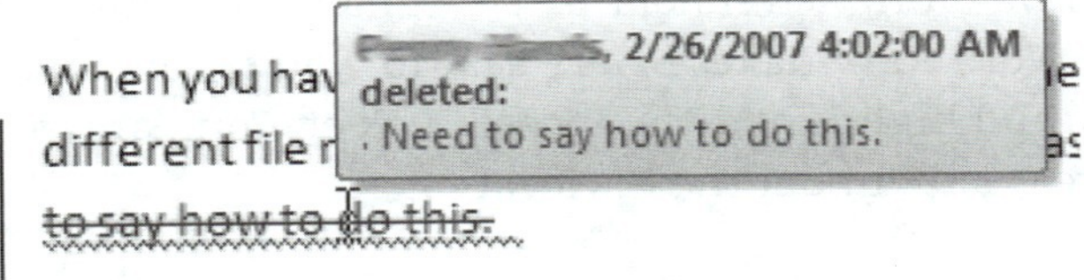

Track Changes in Print Layout view, showing formatting changes in the markup column at the right-hand side, without using the Reviewing Pane:

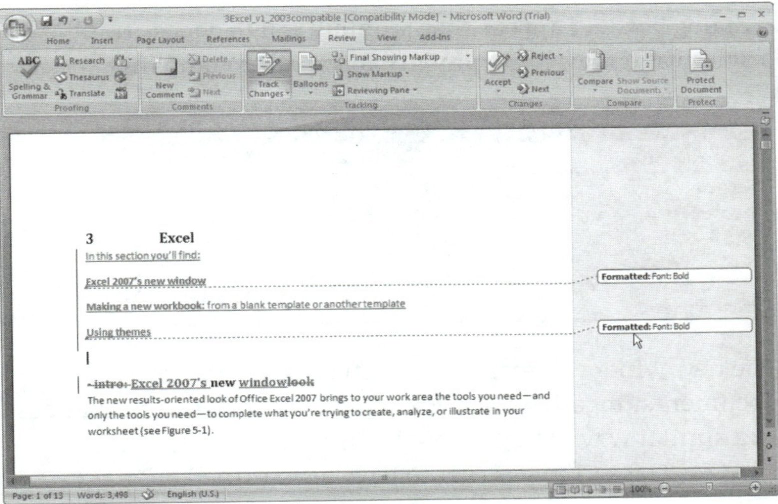

Track Changes in the same view, but using the Reviewing Pane:

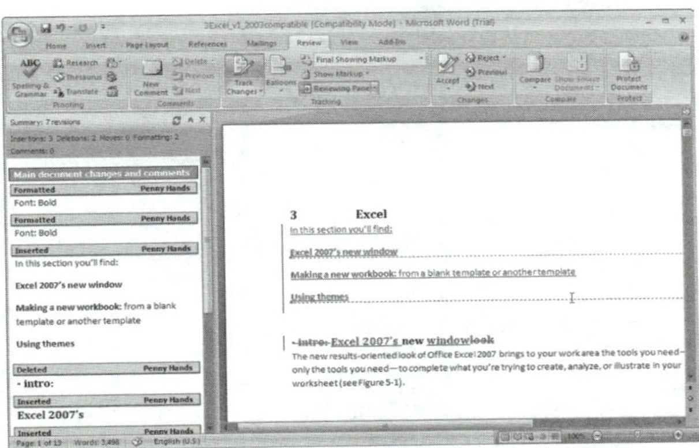

Document comparison

When you have multiple versions of a document with different file names, Word 2007 makes it very easy for you to compare the versions and highlight differences. Click on Compare in the Compare group, under the Review tab:

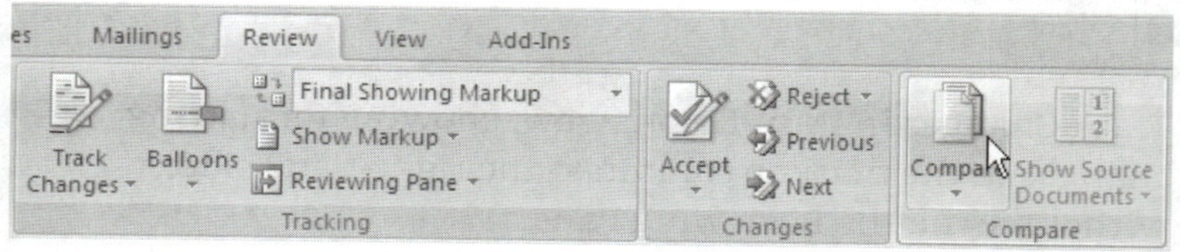

A dialog box will appear that prompts you to choose the original and revised documents you wish to compare:

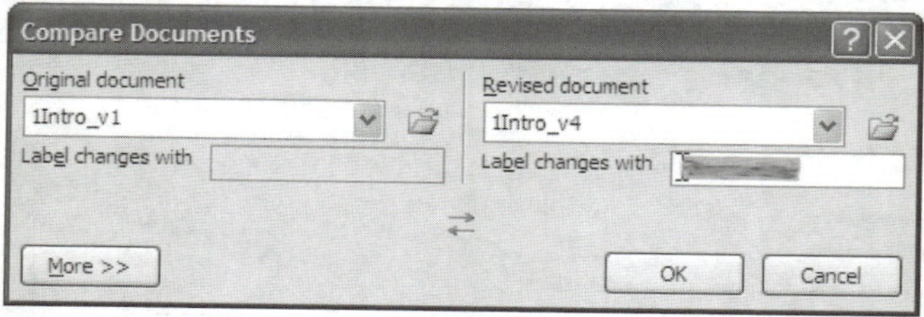

The new window created when you click OK shows both documents, together with a merged version showing changes in a similar way to that of Track Changes, but without the need for Track Changes ever to have been turned on:

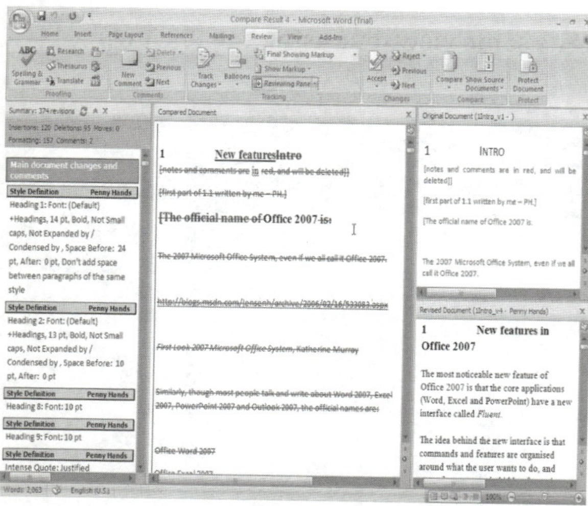

This enables you to review the merged version and the original and revised versions of the document at the same time.

Blogging from Word

Word 2007 makes it easy to post directly to a blog, giving you the advantages of using spelling and grammar tools, SmartArt, easy insertion of graphics and photos, etc.

To do this, choose the Blog template when creating a new document and then create your post:

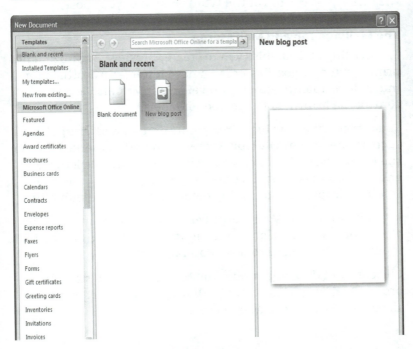

The first time you try to publish a post, Word 2007 will prompt you for your blog's location and your log-in details. If you do not already have a compatible blog, Word 2007 will provide you with information on suitable blogs and how to register.

The blog template's Ribbon is simpler, with only three main tabs, Blog, Insert and Add-Ins:

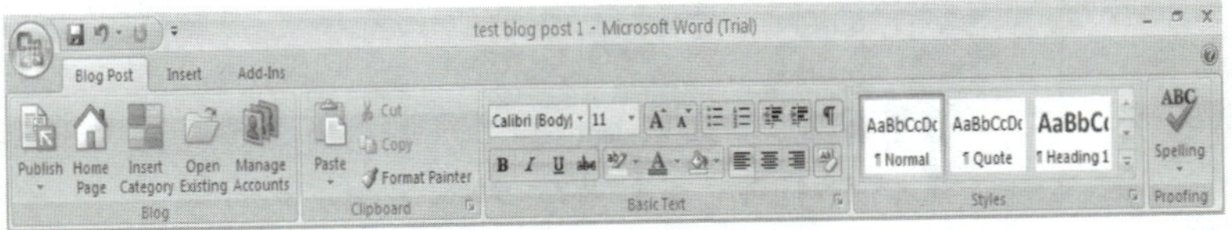

Just as when working with a regular Word 2007 document, clicking on a graphic object will make the Format tab (with Picture Styles and Arrange groups, etc) appear:

If you manage to publish your post successfully, Word records the fact across the top of the Word version of your post.

The Mailings Tab and Mail Merge

The Mailings tab enables you to create, preview, organize, and print a letter (or possibly email a newsletter, etc) destined for multiple recipients, quickly and efficiently. It also lets you control the printing of envelopes or labels.

You can create a new list of recipients or use an existing list, such as one in your Outlook Address Book. Mail Merge will use the list to insert names and addresses into multiple letters/envelopes/labels when it comes to printing, saving you the trouble of copying and pasting details for these individually.

If you haven't used Mail Merge before, use a built-in letter (or other) template and a short recipient list the first time you try it out, just to get used to how Mail Merge works.

Click Start Mail Merge, under the Mailings tab, to start the process and, unless already familiar with all the required steps, choose the Mail Merge wizard:

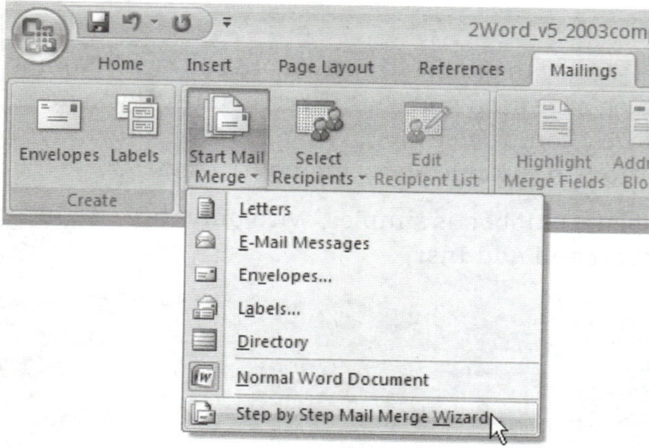

The wizard guides you through all the necessary steps in the process, from choosing the sort of document you want to send all the way through to printing or emailing:

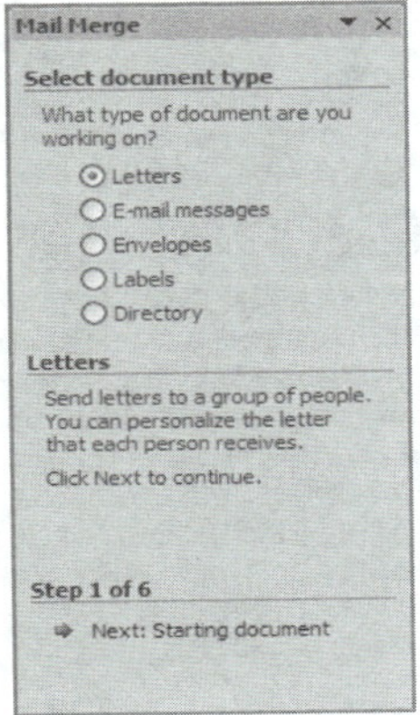

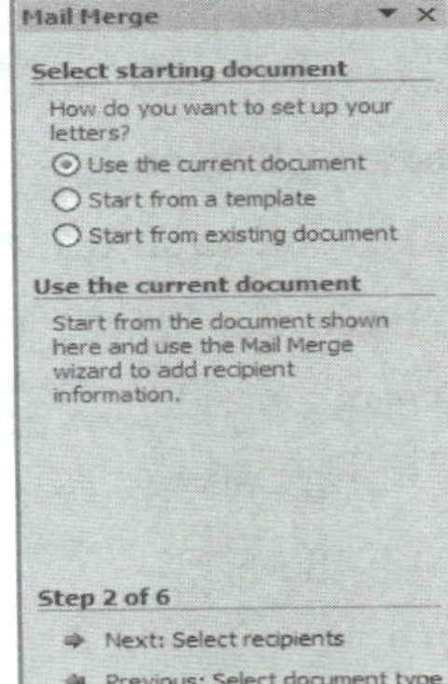

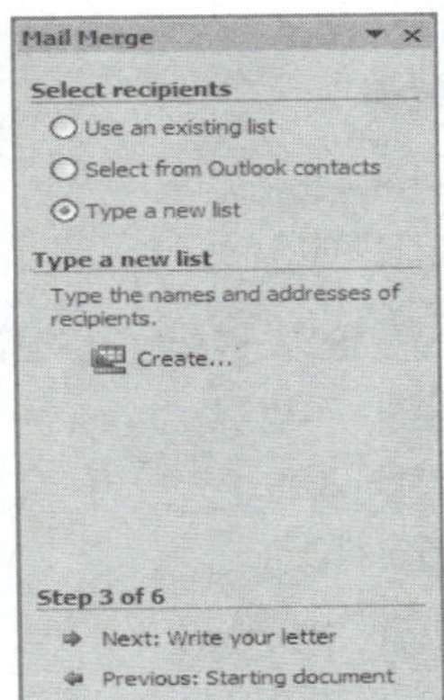

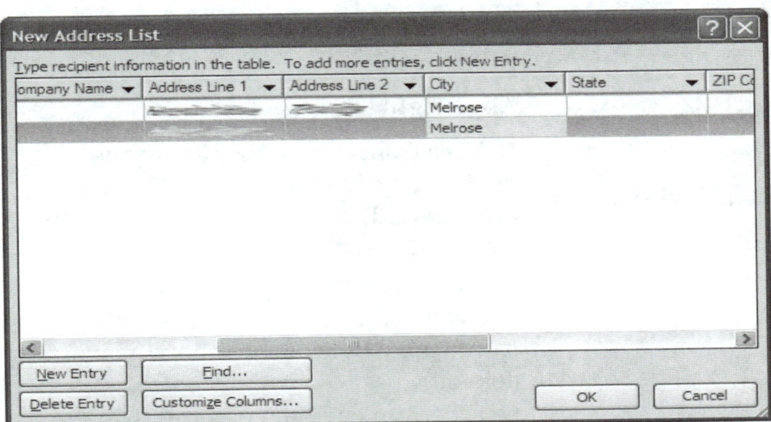

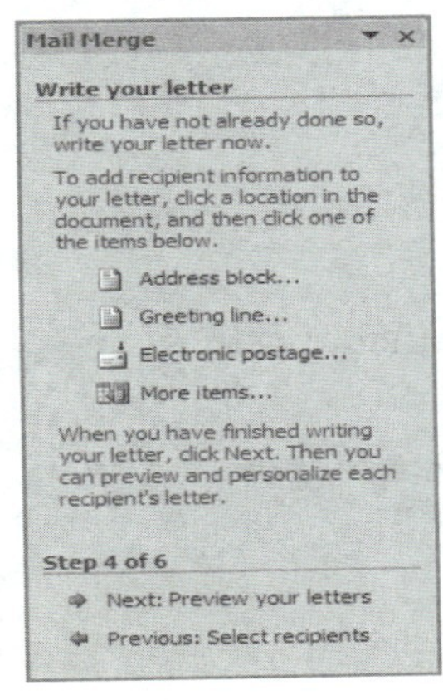

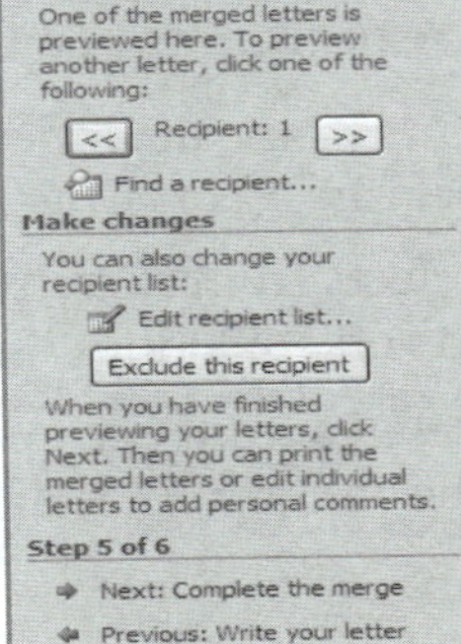

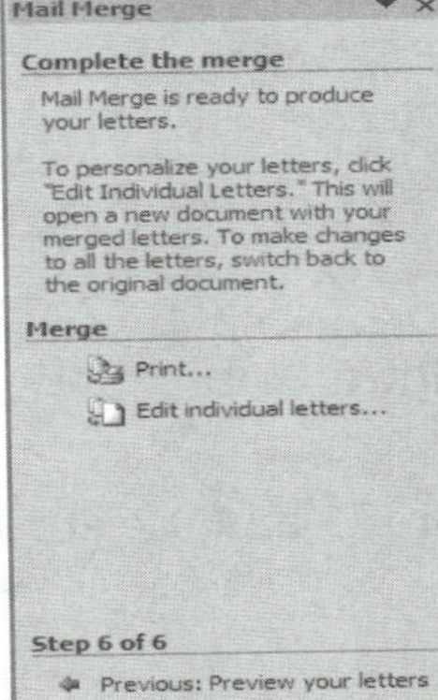

Keyboard shortcuts for Word 2007

You can use all the keyboard shortcuts for formatting that worked in previous versions of Word 2007.

Shortcut	Command
Ctrl+B	makes selection bold
Ctrl+I	makes selection italic
Ctrl+U	makes selection underlined
Ctrl+Shift+A	Uppercase
Ctrl+Alt+1	Heading 1 style
Ctrl+Alt+2	Heading 2 style
Ctrl+Alt+3	Heading 3 style
Ctrl+Shift+N	Normal style
Ctrl+E	Align centre
Ctrl+J	Justify
Ctrl+L	Align left
Ctrl+R	Align right
Ctrl+Backspace	Deletes from cursor position to the beginning of a word (if cursor is in space after a word, the whole of the previous word is deleted)
Ctrl+Delete	Deletes from cursor position to the end of a word (if cursor is in space before a word, the whole of the following word is deleted)
Shift+Home	Selects from current cursor position to the beginning of a line
Shift+Home, Delete	Deletes from current cursor position to the beginning of a line
Shift+Home, Ctrl+X	Cuts from current cursor position to the beginning of a line
Shift+End	Selects from current cursor position to the end of a line
Shift+ End, Delete	Deletes from current cursor position to the end of a line

Quick Tips

Formatting

Formatting options such as Bold, Italic, Font color, Align to left or right, Bullets and Numbering and Styles are found in the Home tab. For further options, click on the dialog launcher in the bottom right-hand corner of any command set.

Quick formatting is available via the Mini Toolbar that pops up when text is selected:

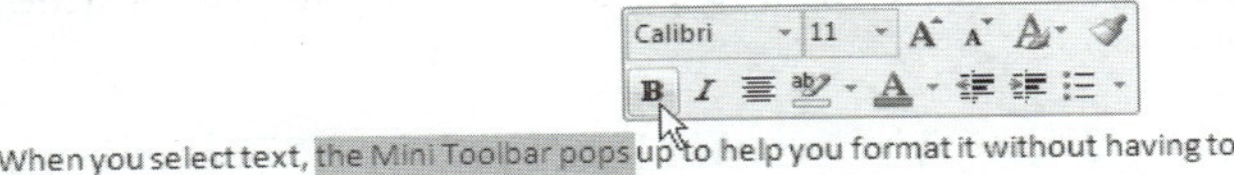
Calibri
11
When you select text, the Mini Toolbar pops up to help you format it without having to

Saving

To save, go to the Office menu and click on Save (or press S) or press Ctrl+S (without opening the menu). To Save As, click on the Office Button and choose Save As or simply press F12 at any time.

Lists

To apply bullets and numbering styles, use the new Bullet Library and Numbering Library. To do this, click on the small down-arrow in the Bullets or Numbering options in the Home tab. This will display all available options.

Inserting symbols and special characters

To find symbols and other non-standard characters that are not on the keyboard, go to the Insert tab and click on the Symbol command in the Symbols command set.

Find and Replace

Go to the Home tab and click on Find to carry out a simple search for an item, or Replace to find an item and replace it with another. Alternatively, press Ctrl+F to open the Find & Replace dialog box.

Footnotes and endnotes

To add a footnote or an endnote, go to the References tab and click on Insert Footnote or Insert Endnote.

2 • Microsoft® Office Excel® 2007

Microsoft® Office Excel® 2007's new window

As with other major Office Professional 2007 system applications, Office Excel 2007's new Fluent user interface is designed to help you be more productive by organizing many commonly-used commands under tabs in the Ribbon, as well as under contextual tabs when carrying out specific operations (such as printing) or when particular objects in your worksheet are selected.

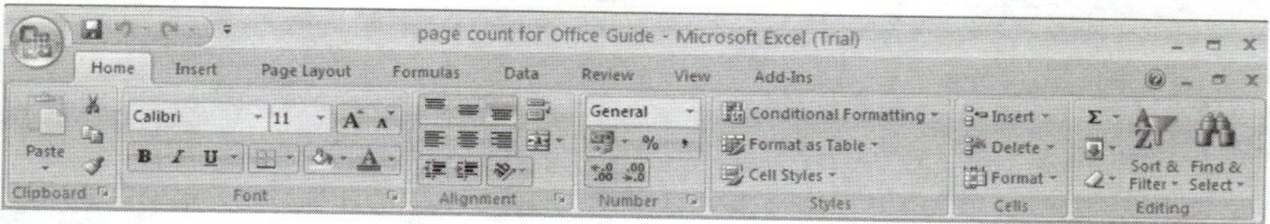

The Home tab includes the commands you need to work with the Clipboard: choose and change fonts, control the alignment of cell content, select number formats, choose cell style and format, and edit, sort, and search your data.

The Insert tab houses the commands for the objects you add to your worksheets, for example: tables, charts, illustrations, links, and various kinds of text items such as column or row labels.

The Page Layout tab offers all things related to setting up the worksheet, including choosing themes, selecting page setup options, controlling the scaling of individual objects, selecting worksheet options, and arranging items on the sheet.

The Formulas tab includes the Function Wizard, the Function Library, the commands you need for creating and working with named cells, commands for formula auditing, and calculation options.

The Data tab offers commands for getting external data, managing the connections to external links, sorting and filtering your data, removing duplicates, validating and consolidating your data, and grouping and ungrouping cells.

The Review tab includes options to proof, comment on, share and protect the sheet.

The View tab provides commands for choosing different

workbook views, hiding and redisplaying worksheet elements (gridlines, the ruler, the formula bar, and more), magnifying or reducing the display, and working with the worksheet window.

Excel 2007 is much more powerful than previous versions. It can handle worksheets with enormous amounts of data, over 16,000 columns and more than 1,000,000 rows. It also has enhanced formatting and charting abilities and in this section you can see some of the features that help you create professional-looking worksheets.

Templates, themes and cell styles

When you make a new workbook by clicking the Office Button and choosing New from the Office menu, the New Workbook window offers you a comprehensive list of template categories to choose from:

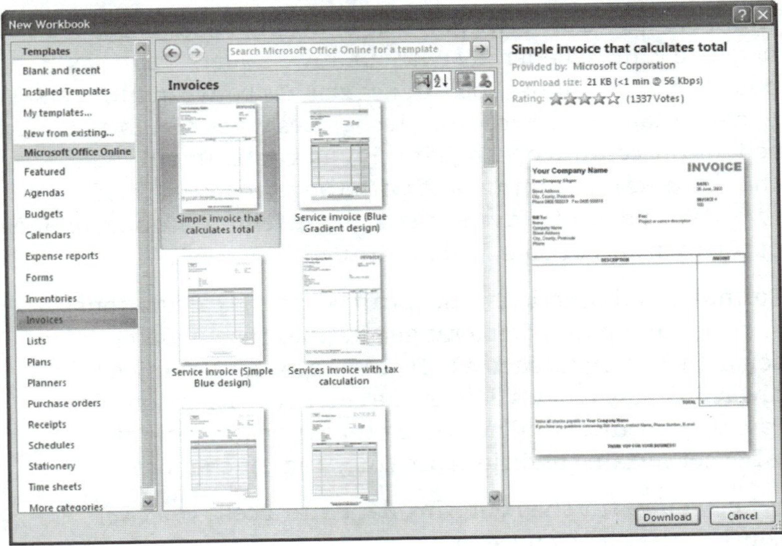

Think of templates as starter documents that already have a theme and use fonts, colours and other attributes (e.g. types of border and shading) that go together well. Naturally, many templates also already have useful built-in functions (such as for today's date) and formulas for particular ranges of cells, and, even if a template is not exactly what you need, you can often find something that approximates what you would like and adapt it for your own purposes.

The New Workbook window makes it very easy for you to browse template categories online as well as installed templates. If you find an online template you'd like to use, click the Download button and after an automated validation check a new workbook is created, based on the template.

If you'd rather start your new workbook from scratch, you can choose the blank template from the New Workbook menu (or Crl+N as a shortcut).

Entering data and navigating

Click on any cell to start entering data into it. Data can be text, numbers or formulas.

Text: could be titles, descriptions, labels such as 'year', 'month', 'income', etc, or could be text and number combinations (which still count as text) such as 'Q1 Sales', '2006 accounts', etc.

Numbers: these are always whole or decimal positive or negative values, generally without any characters such as pound or dollar signs. You can use slashes between numbers to create dates that Excel 2007 recognizes when you format a cell, or the column or range it is in, as a date. It will then turn the value we enter into a date with the format we specify, e.g. 27/2/07 could be displayed as 27/2/07; 27 February, 2007, or one of the many other date formats available in Excel.

Formulas and functions: these can be simple calculations, such as adding together a range of values, useful date-sensitive functions such as =TODAY() or =YEAR() which will always display today's date or the current year, or complex calculations involving multiple ranges of data, tests of whether certain conditions are true, and much more.

When you've finished entering data into a cell, you can confirm the fact by pressing:

• Enter (which takes you to the next cell down, ready to enter more data there)

• Arrow key (taking you to the cell immediately above, below, left or right of the current cell, depending which arrow key you press)

• Tab (taking you to the next cell to the right, in the same row as the current cell)

- Shift+Tab (taking you to the cell immediately to the left)

Alternatively (unless the current cell has a formula you've been editing) you can use the mouse and click on any other cell. Cells with formulas that involve other cells or a range are sensitive (until you confirm that you've finished editing them) to clicking in other cells, taking that to mean that you want that cell to be included in the formula. Rather than click in another cell, you can confirm a formula by using the keyboard, as above, or by clicking the tick that represents Enter in the formula bar:

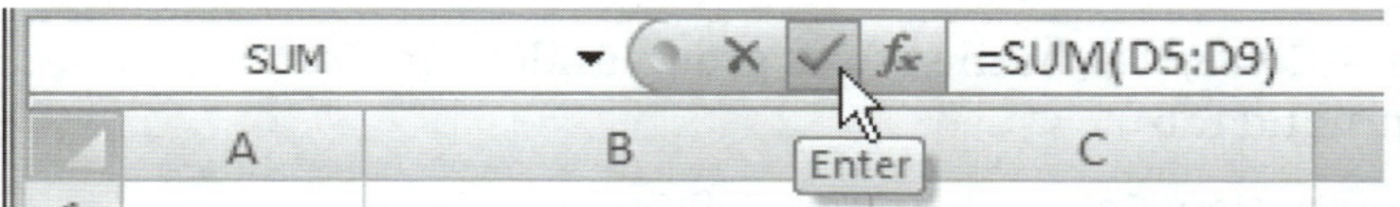

Using AutoFill to enter data

You can use AutoFill to enter data that follows any sort of pattern. Try entering data into the first two cells of the range you'd like to use AutoFill on (or even only the first cell if the progression is an obvious one such as 1 to 10 or Jan to Dec), then drag over the two cells to select them and position the mouse pointer over the bottom-right corner of the second cell (where you'll see a small square) so that it changes into a smaller, solid black, cross-shaped mouse pointer. This is known as the fill handle. Click on the fill handle and drag it outside the selection over the rest of the range (Excel 2007 gives you a preview of the result in a tool tip) and release the mouse button to confirm:

	A	B	C
10			
11	item	ex VAT price	price with VAT
12	bg 24	32.5	
13	xk 345	125.95	
14	d32	8.75	
15	amx-64	25	
16	cat 35 t1	29.99	
17	cat 35 t2	39.99	
18	cat 35 t3		
19	cat 35 t4		
20	cat 35 t5		

	A	B	C
10			
11	item	ex VAT price	price with VAT
12	bg 24	32.5	
13	xk 345	125.95	
14	d32	8.75	
15	amx-64	25	
16	cat 35 t1	29.99	
17	cat 35 t2	39.99	
18	cat 35 t3		
19	cat 35 t4		
20	cat 35 t5		69.99
21			

	A	B	C
10			
11	item	ex VAT price	price with VAT
12	bg 24	32.5	
13	xk 345	125.95	
14	d32	8.75	
15	amx-64	25	
16	cat 35 t1	29.99	
17	cat 35 t2	39.99	
18	cat 35 t3	49.99	
19	cat 35 t4	59.99	
20	cat 35 t5	69.99	
21			

Formatting

You can apply predesigned formats to selected cells or ranges by clicking Cell Styles, in the Styles group under the Home command tab, and choosing the type of formatting from the gallery that appears.

The Cell Styles gallery also contains options for different types of number format, such as currency and percentage.

Tip: You can create formats for your own cell styles and add them to the gallery.

- apply the format you want to a specific cell
- click Cell Styles in the Styles group under the Home command tab
- choose New Cell Style in the Cell Styles gallery
- review the information in the Style dialog box and click Format if you need to make any changes
- type a name for the style in the Style Name field, then click OK to save the style

The new style you created appears at the top of the gallery in the Custom category. If you ever want to delete your custom style from the gallery, right-click on it within the gallery and select Delete.

Formulas and functions

Formulas perform calculations on the contents of one or more cells.

For example, to add cell A1 and cell C9 together and show the result in cell D3, we would click on D3 and type:

=A1+C9

Order of precedence

Excel 2007 observes an order of precedence in formulas: multiply, divide, add, subtract.

This means that it will multiply elements in a formula before it divides, and will then go on to any adding or subtracting required. This is an essential basic fact to be remembered and understood in order to avoid baffling results in complex formulas. For example:

Formula	What it means
=A10-D4*E4	multiply the value in D4 by that in E4 and subtract the result from the value in A10

e.g. if A10 is 5, D4 is 2 and E4 is 3, the result is -1

Using parentheses

If you'd actually like to subtract D4 from A10 and multiply the result by E4, you should use one of these formulas instead:

=(A10-D4)*E4 or =E4*(A10-D4)

e.g. if A10 is 5, D4 is 2 and E4 is 3, the result is 9

To work out the VAT (at 17.5%) that should be applied to an item with an ex-VAT price in cell E7, you could use this formula:
=E7*17.5%

To calculate the price including VAT, you could use this formula:
= E7*17.5%+ E7

But it's probably as easy to just multiply by 1.175 in a basic, quick calculation:
= E7*1.175

Absolute references: using $

If, however, you want to see what prices would be with different rates of VAT, you could put the rate of VAT in a cell of its own (say D5) and reference that in your formula:
=E7*D5+E7

By putting the value in one cell, and basing all formulas for individual calculations on the value of that single cell, you can type different values for the rate of VAT in just that cell and see the effects in all the calculations based on it. For this to work, the reference to the cell in each of the individual formulas must be an absolute reference (one that doesn't change when copied from a cell and pasted elsewhere) rather than a conventional one (which is relative, and does change when pasted).

The dollar signs make the reference absolute (people also refer to the reference being 'anchored') so that if, for example, you put your formula in F7, to calculate the price including VAT of an item with an ex-VAT price in E7, and have a range of other ex-VAT prices in column E from E8 to E15, you can copy and paste (or autofill) the formula all the way down column F without the D5 reference changing:

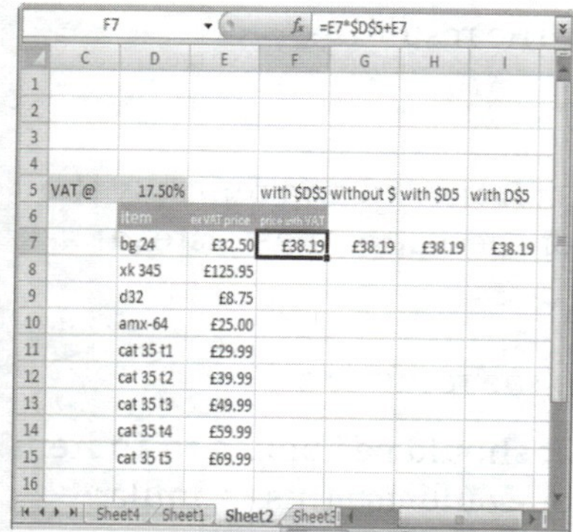

F7 | =E7*D5+E7

	C	D	E	F	G	H	I
5	VAT @	17.50%		with D5	without $	with $D5	with D$5
6		item	ex VAT price	price with VAT			
7		bg 24	£32.50	£38.19	£38.19	£38.19	£38.19
8		xk 345	£125.95				
9		d32	£8.75				
10		amx-64	£25.00				
11		cat 35 t1	£29.99				
12		cat 35 t2	£39.99				
13		cat 35 t3	£49.99				
14		cat 35 t4	£59.99				
15		cat 35 t5	£69.99				

Sheet4 Sheet1 Sheet2 Sheet3

F7 | =E7*D5+E7

	C	D	E	F	G	H	I
5	VAT @	17.50%		with D5	without $	with $D5	with D$5
6		item	ex VAT price	price with VAT			
7		bg 24	£32.50	£38.19	£38.19	£38.19	£38.19
8		xk 345	£125.95	£147.99			
9		d32	£8.75	£10.28			
10		amx-64	£25.00	£29.38			
11		cat 35 t1	£29.99	£35.24			
12		cat 35 t2	£39.99	£46.99			
13		cat 35 t3	£49.99	£58.74			
14		cat 35 t4	£59.99	£70.49			
15		cat 35 t5	£69.99	£82.24			

Sheet4 Sheet1 Sheet2 Sheet3

The formula in cell F15 would therefore be =E15*D5+E15, whereas if you copied and pasted =E15*D5+E15 to the same range, F8:F15, it would be =E15*D13+E15 in F15. Here's an example of that faulty formula used in column F:

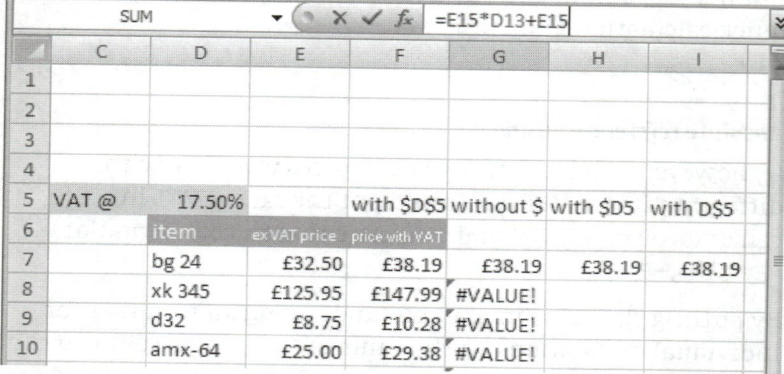

SUM | =E15*D13+E15

	C	D	E	F	G	H	I
5	VAT @	17.50%		with D5	without $	with $D5	with D$5
6		item	ex VAT price	price with VAT			
7		bg 24	£32.50	£38.19	£38.19	£38.19	£38.19
8		xk 345	£125.95	£147.99	#VALUE!		
9		d32	£8.75	£10.28	#VALUE!		
10		amx-64	£25.00	£29.38	#VALUE!		

The lack of the dollar sign causes the D5 reference to change from cell to cell in the range, in the same way as the E7 reference. This would mean that only one calculation (the one in row 7) would work. All the other formulas in the range would fail due to an empty reference, because the cells D6:D13 do not have a percentage to use in the calculation.

By using $ to create an absolute reference to D5 in all the formulas in the range F7:F15, you can change the VAT value in just one cell (D5) and see the effect of the change on the prices of all your products.

Using AutoFill to add formulas to a range

Rather than using copy and paste, it's often easier to use AutoFill to fill a range with formulas. Type the formula into the first cell in the range and then drag the fill handle to fill the range:

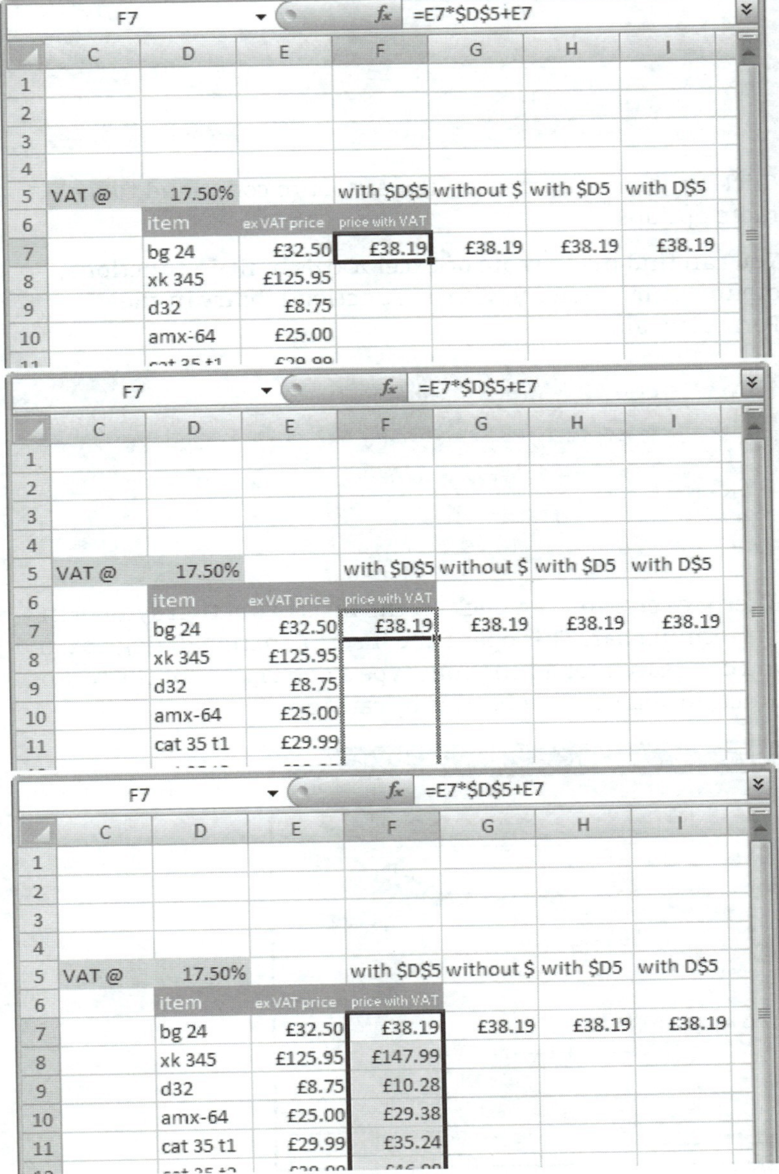

Functions are very useful, such as for automatically adding a range of cells (AutoSum), displaying the current year, etc.

AutoSum is probably the most used function. To use it, click in the cell where you would like the total of a range of values to appear and then click on the AutoSum command in the Function Library, within the Formulas tab:

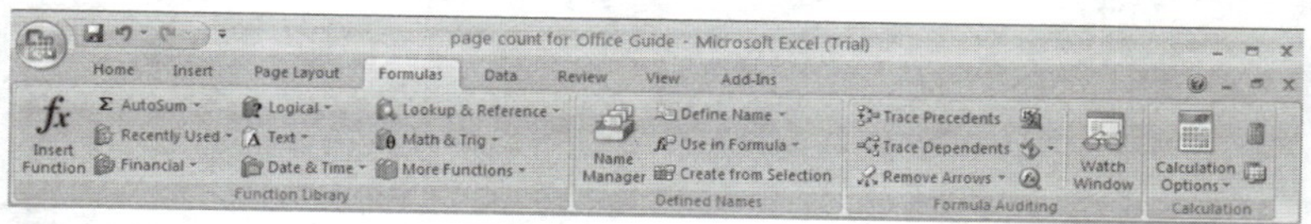

Click on the more arrow on the AutoSum command to see more options.

You can find many more of Excel 2007's built-in functions, organized by category, via the Function Library in the Formulas tab:

Alternatively, you can click on the Insert Function symbol in the formula bar. This opens the Insert Function dialog box and you can search for a function, type a description of the sort of function you need, or browse by category:

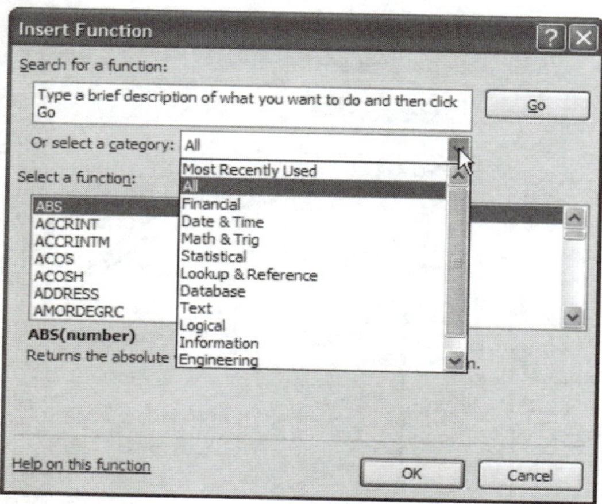

When you select a function, a useful description is provided of its use. If you think a function might be what you want, but you're still unsure as to what it does, you can select it in the Insert Function window and click on the Help on this function link in the bottom-left corner.

Another way to access functions, if a cell already has a function you would like to change, is to click within the cell with the function (as if to start editing it) and then click on the down arrow next to the current function in the name box in the formula bar:

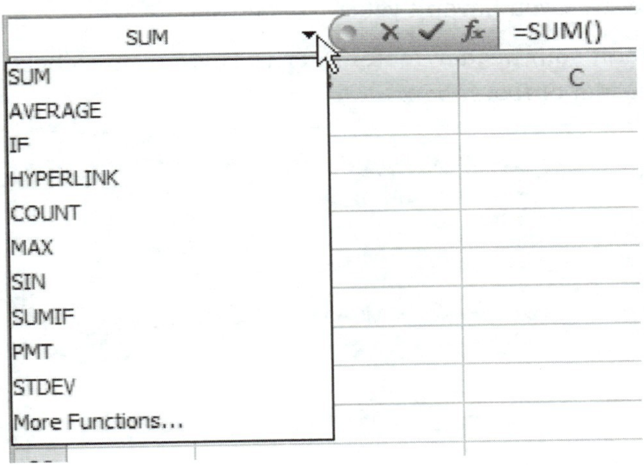

Page Layout view and printing

Page Layout view (new in Excel 2007) lets you see, while you're working on it, how your worksheet should look when it is printed. Page Layout view is not just a preview — everything is fully editable.

You can switch to Page Layout view either by clicking the View tab and selecting Page Layout View or by clicking Page Layout in the Quick Views control in the bottom-right of the window:

You can use the Zoom control to zoom out and view multiple pages in Page Layout view:

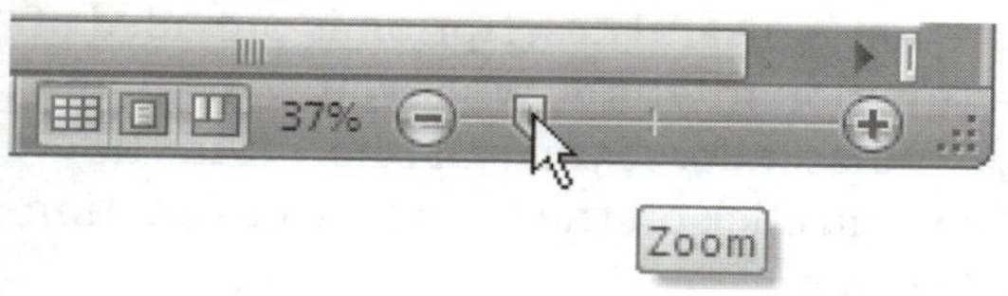

Headers and footers

You can insert and edit headers and footers by clicking on Header & Footer under the Insert tab. Alternatively, simply go to the Print Layout view. This always displays boxes for header and footer, even if you haven't yet created either.

To create or edit your header/footer in Print Layout view, click inside the header or footer box:

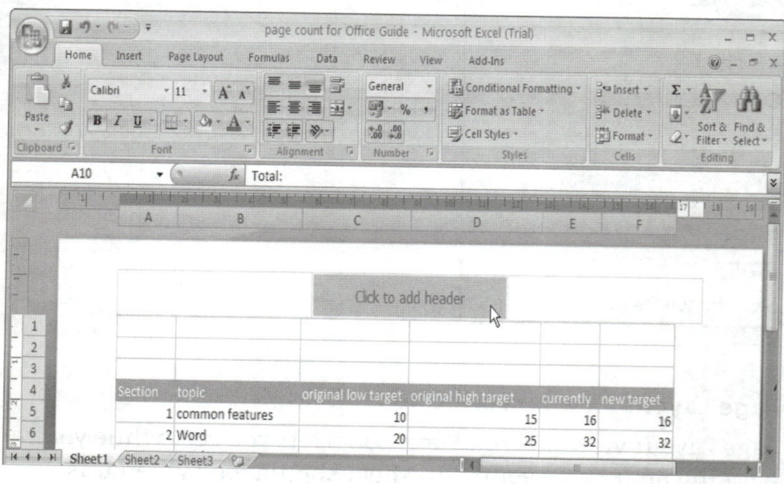

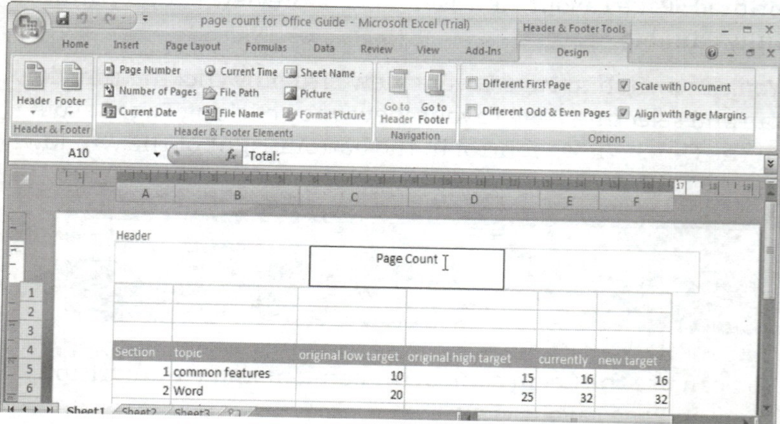

As soon as you click inside the header or footer box, the Design contextual tab appears on the Ribbon, with relevant Header & Footer tools:

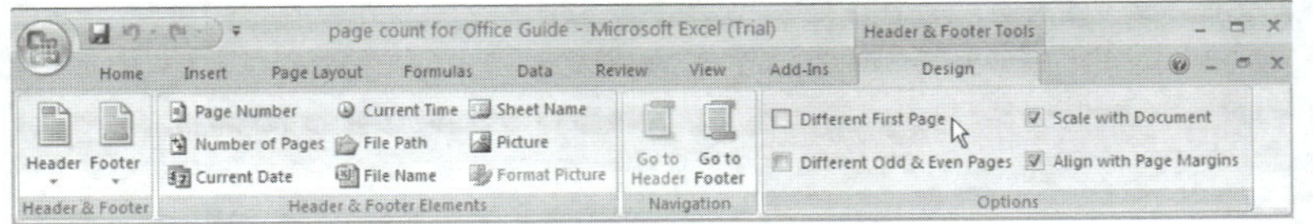

The Header and Footer commands under the Design tab showing the context-sensitive Header & Footer tools (these tools only appear when you click within a header or footer box) provide suggestions for ready-made headers and footers, using elements such as author name, document name, date, page number, file name and location, etc.

Charts

Charts help you to illustrate in a colourful and understandable way, what the information in your sheet's data means.

Start by selecting the data range(s) you want to chart. Then click the Insert tab and choose the chart type you want to create:

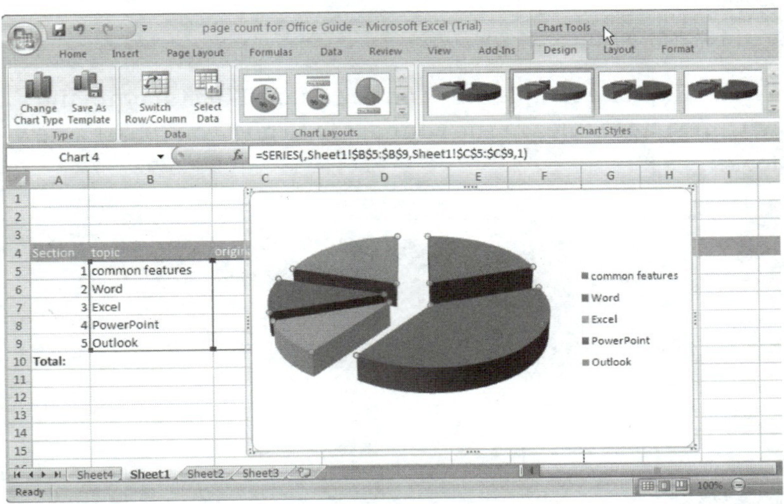

The chart appears on your worksheet, and the Chart Tools contextual tab offers three full sets of options for customizing your charts:

• The Design tab gives you choices for selecting the chart type, data source and arrangement, Quick Layout, Quick Styles, and the Move Chart command:

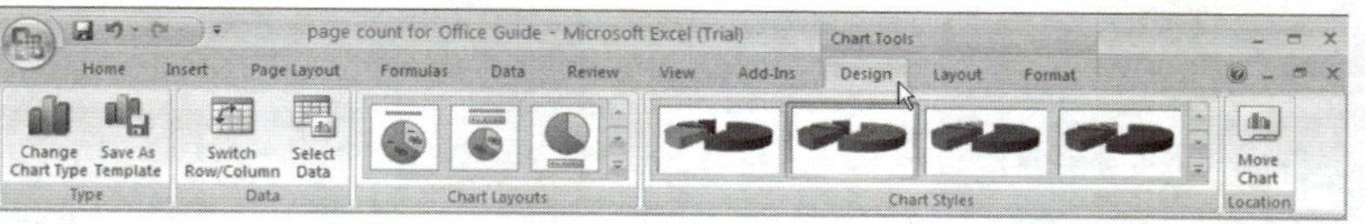

• The Layout tab in Chart Tools enables you to enter chart properties, choose Office Shapes, add or edit chart elements, and make choices related to 3-D charts:

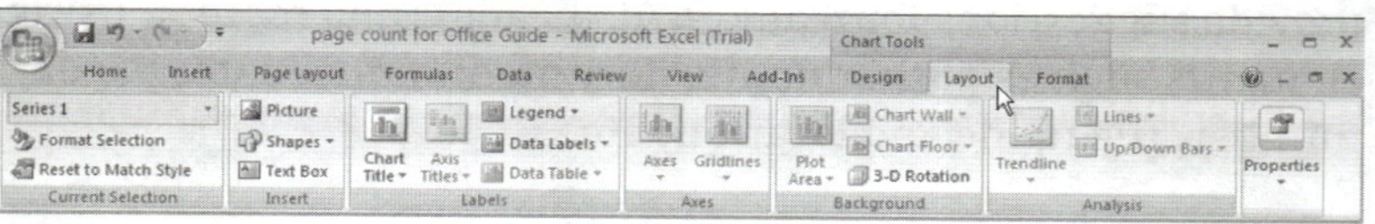

• The Format tab lets you select different chart elements and add styles to the chart shape, such as 3-D edges, shadows, bevel, etc:

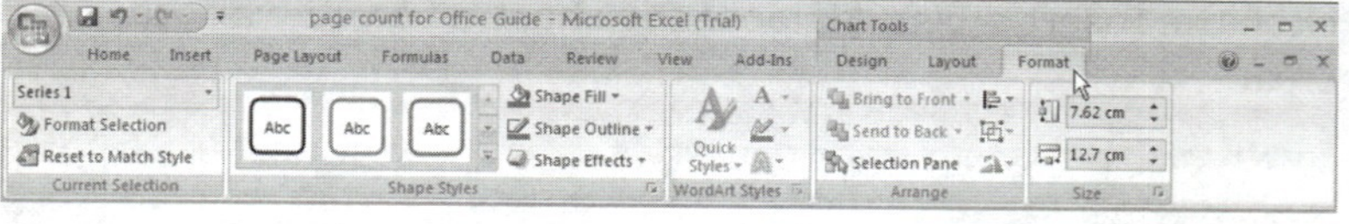

You could, for example, click on the Shape Effects command within Shape Styles in the Format tab to give your chart a new look:

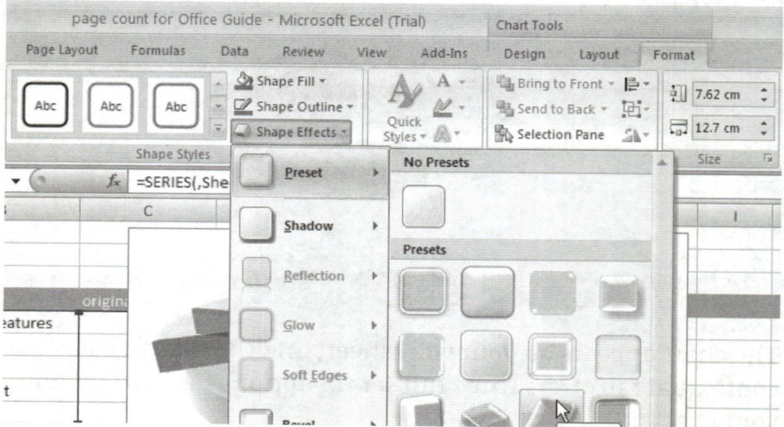

Shapes, WordArt and SmartArt

Shapes (the lines, rectangles, block arrows, etc, that used to be situated in the Drawing toolbar) now have their own space within the Insert tab. To see the expanded collection of shapes, click the Shapes command in the Illustrations group:

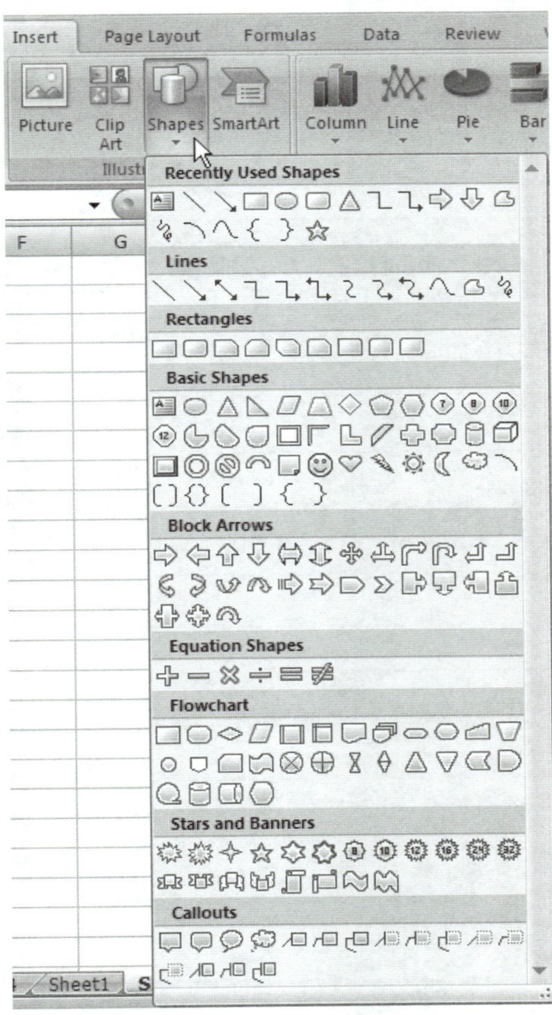

WordArt is now accessible via the Text group of the Insert tab. When you choose the WordArt command, a gallery of styles appears. Click the one you want and the WordArt item is placed on your worksheet. Click the item to replace it with your own text:

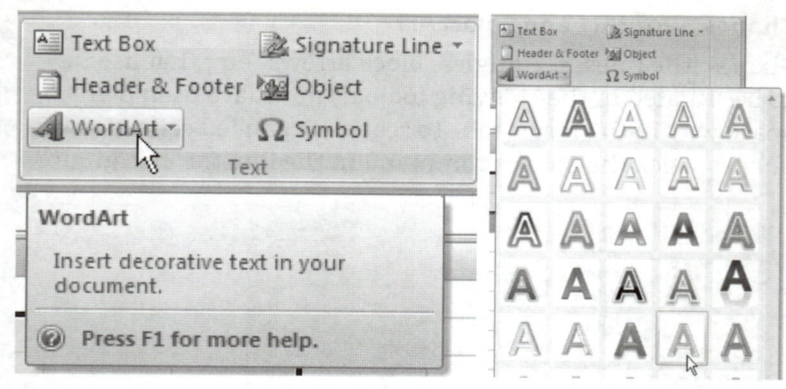

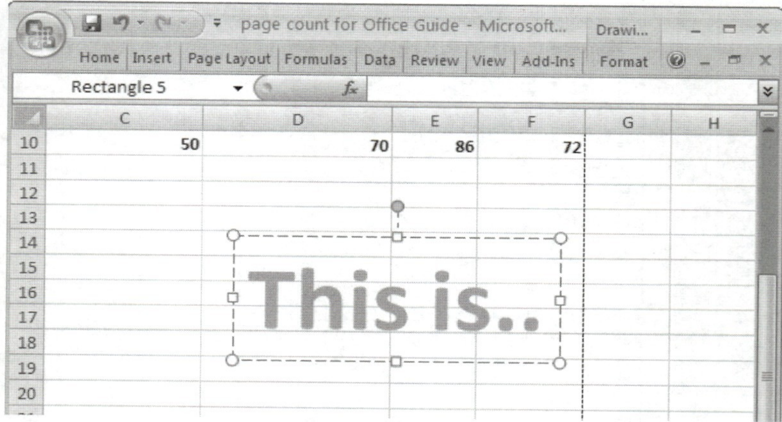

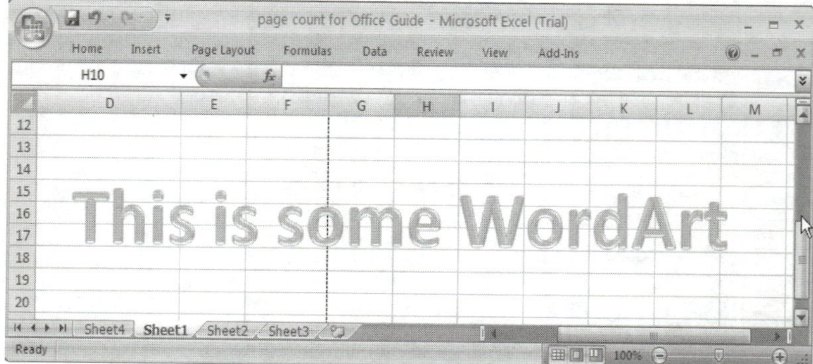

To create SmartArt graphics, open the Insert tab and click SmartArt in the Illustrations command set. Then select the diagram type you want to create, choose the style you prefer, and click OK:

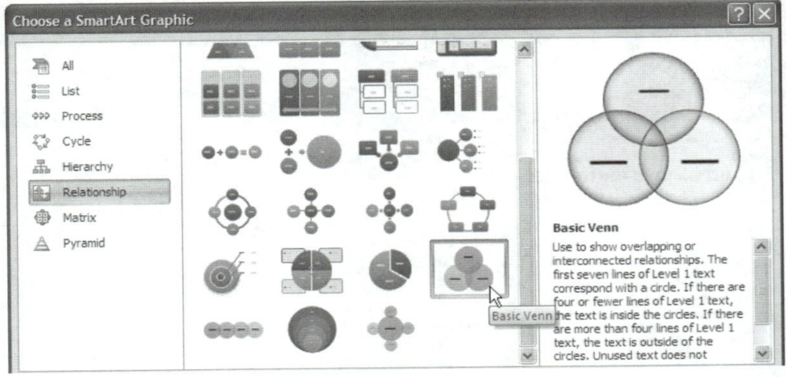

Conditional Formatting and Data Visualizations

Conditional formatting lets you apply specific formatting to cells according to the value of a cell or the value of a formula. For example, you could colour code a set of exam results according to whether marks were higher than a particular value or not, and so label fails as red and passes as green:

	A	B	C	D	E
1	**Winter Semester Results**				
2		student id no	written	oral	combined
3	*points available*		*70*	*30*	*100*
4	pass mark = greater than:		35	14	49
5		07ws01	49	24	73
6		07ws02	30	15	45
7		07ws03	27	28	55
8		07ws04	44	12	56
9		07ws05	54	13	67
10		07ws06	25	25	50
11		07ws07	34	11	45
12		07ws08	61	12	73
13		07ws09	33	14	47
14		07ws10	47	15	62

To do this, select the range of cells to which you'd like to apply the conditional formatting. Then in the Sheet tab, click Conditional Formatting.

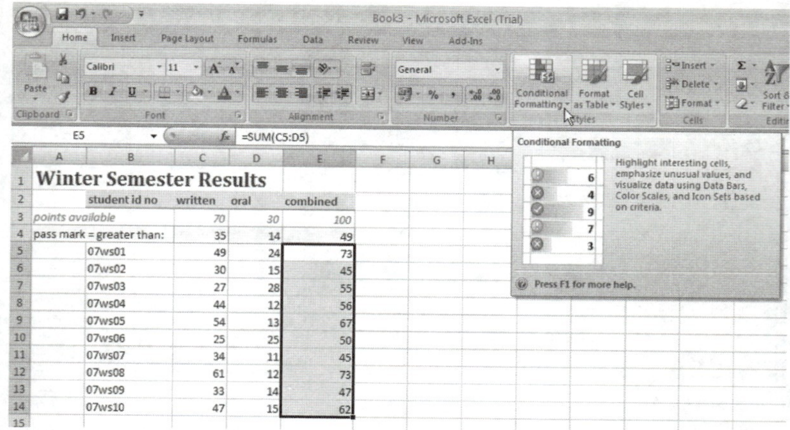

The menu that appears offers two different sets of rules (Highlight Cell Rules and Top/Bottom Rules) that you can apply to your data.

To automatically highlight the cells with a value over 49 (and so label the pass marks in the exam results) we need to identify all the marks in our range that get more than the value in the cell E4 (as 49 or less is a fail). When you point to Highlight Cells Rules such an option becomes obvious in the menu that appears:

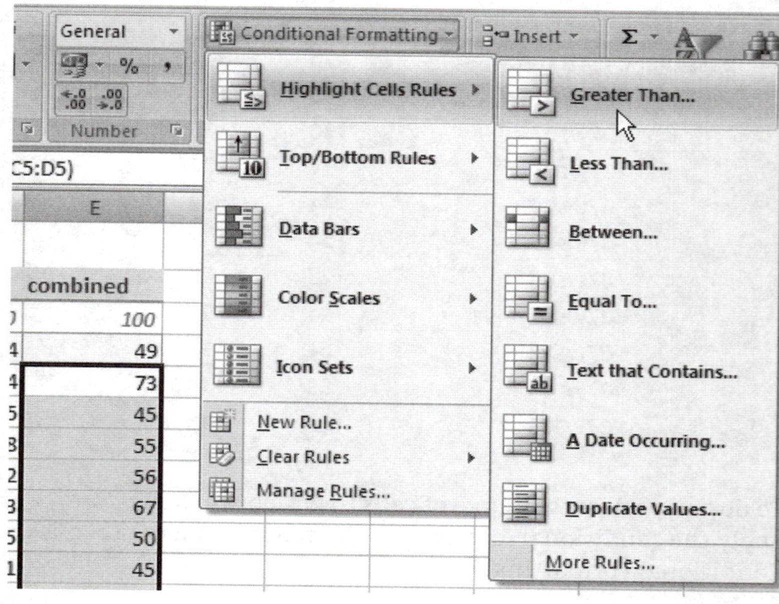

Click on the Greater Than option and then enter the cell reference of the fail mark with an equals sign at the beginning (or just type in 49 if the mark is fixed) and choose a highlighting method (e.g. Green Fill with Dark Green Text) in the dialog box.

As soon as you type a value you can preview the effect of the highlighting. Finally, click OK to save the change and apply the rule you've chosen.

The automatic highlighting appears:

F20

	A	B	C	D	E	F	G
1	**Winter Semester Results**						
2		student id no	written	oral	combined		
3	*points available*		*70*	*30*	*100*		
4	pass mark = greater than:		35	14	49		
5		07ws01	49	24	73		
6		07ws02	30	15	45		
7		07ws03	27	28	55		
8		07ws04	44	12	56		
9		07ws05	54	13	67		
10		07ws06	25	25	50		
11		07ws07	34	11	45		
12		07ws08	61	12	73		
13		07ws09	33	14	47		

To give the other marks a coloured background, select the whole range and fill it with a colour of your choice using the Fill Color tool:

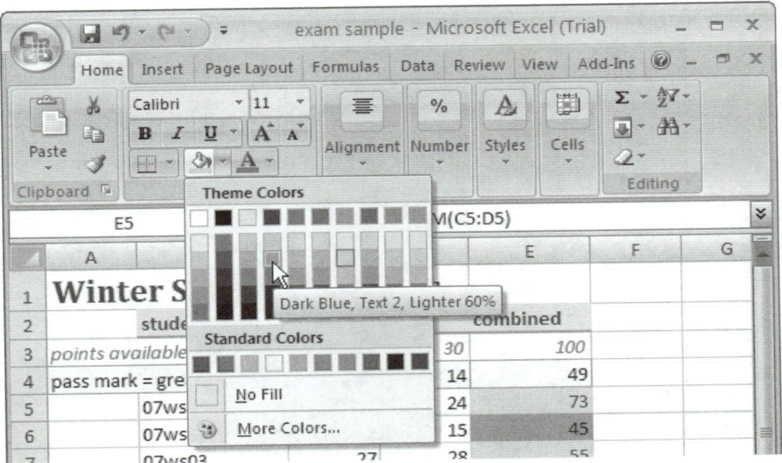

Keyboard shortcuts for Excel 2007

Arrow keys	Go one cell up, down, left or right
Tab	Go one cell to the right
Shift+Tab	Go one cell to the left
Ctrl+arrow key	Go to the edge of the current data region
Ctrl+Home	Go to the beginning of the worksheet
Ctrl+Home	Go to the last occupied cell of the worksheet
Ctrl +Spacebar	Select the entire column
Shift + Spacebar	Select the entire row
Shift +F11	Insert a new worksheet
Ctrl +Page Down	Move to the next sheet in a workbook
Ctrl + Page Up	Move to the previous sheet in a workbook
Shift + Ctrl + Page Down	Select the current and next sheet
Shift + Ctrl + Page Up	Select the current and previous sheet
Alt +E, M	Move or copy the current sheet
Alt+E, L	Delete the current sheet

3 • Microsoft® Office Outlook® 2007

Office Outlook 2007's new features

Office Outlook 2007's main window doesn't share the same new Fluent interface that Microsoft Office Word 2007, Microsoft Office Excel 2007 and Microsoft Office PowerPoint 2007 all have, and its menus (File, Edit, View, Go, Tools, Actions, and Help) and navigation pane should be familiar to anyone who has used earlier versions.

The new Fluent interface is present in some of Office Outlook 2007's windows, such as the New Message window:

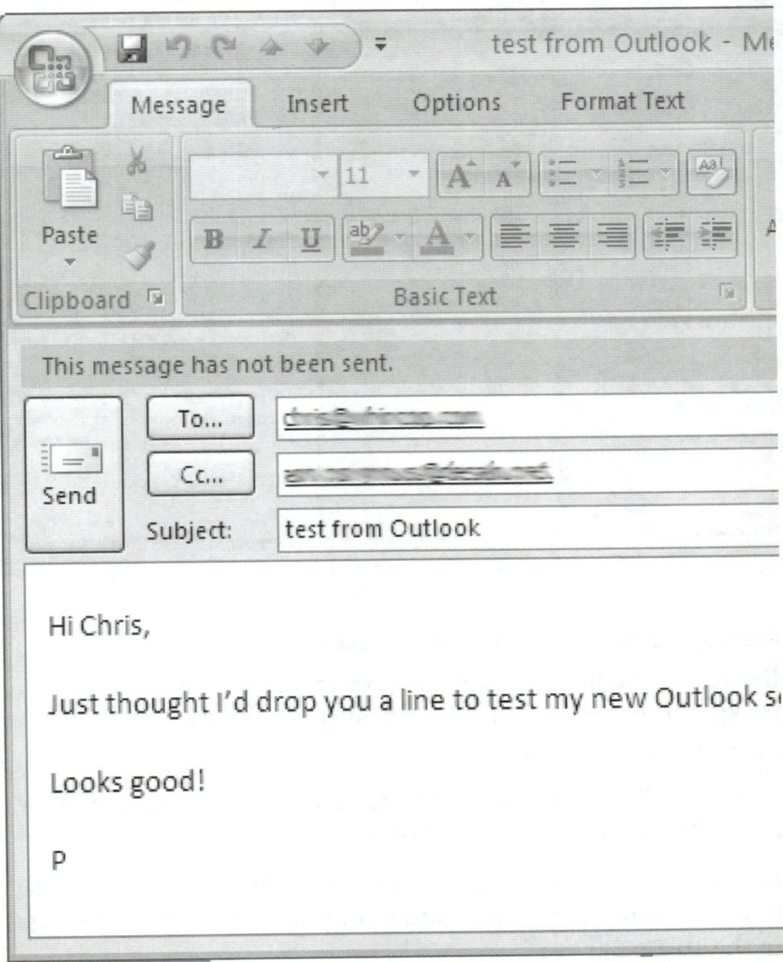

Here are a few of the new features present in the main Outlook 2007 window:

- Search box at the top of the Inbox column
- RSS Feeds folder in the Mail Folders navigation pane
- To-Do Bar along the right side of the window
- Attachment Preview enables you to preview the contents of attachments without opening them

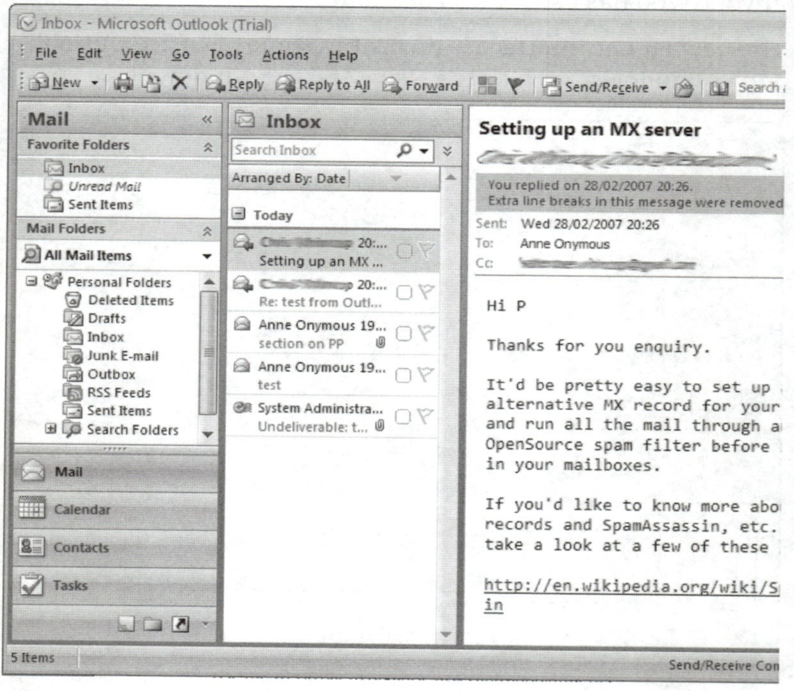

Managing time and organising tasks

Use the To-Do Bar to organise tasks and appointments. It expands when you click on it and shows a calendar, appointments and tasks.

The To-Do Bar is always visible, whether you're working in Mail, Calendar, Contacts or Tasks.

An item is added to the To-Do Bar automatically whenever you flag an email message or contact, or when you drag a message to the To-Do Bar.

Adding tasks to your calendar

Because the Daily Task List displays your tasks in the To-Do Bar according to the day on which they are due, you can easily drag them to your Calendar and then allocate time to complete them. Using the Daily Task List you can also modify the date of tasks by dragging them from one day to another, and the To-Do Bar will update accordingly.

Tasks from the Daily Task List in the To-Do Bar are displayed automatically in the Calendar module:

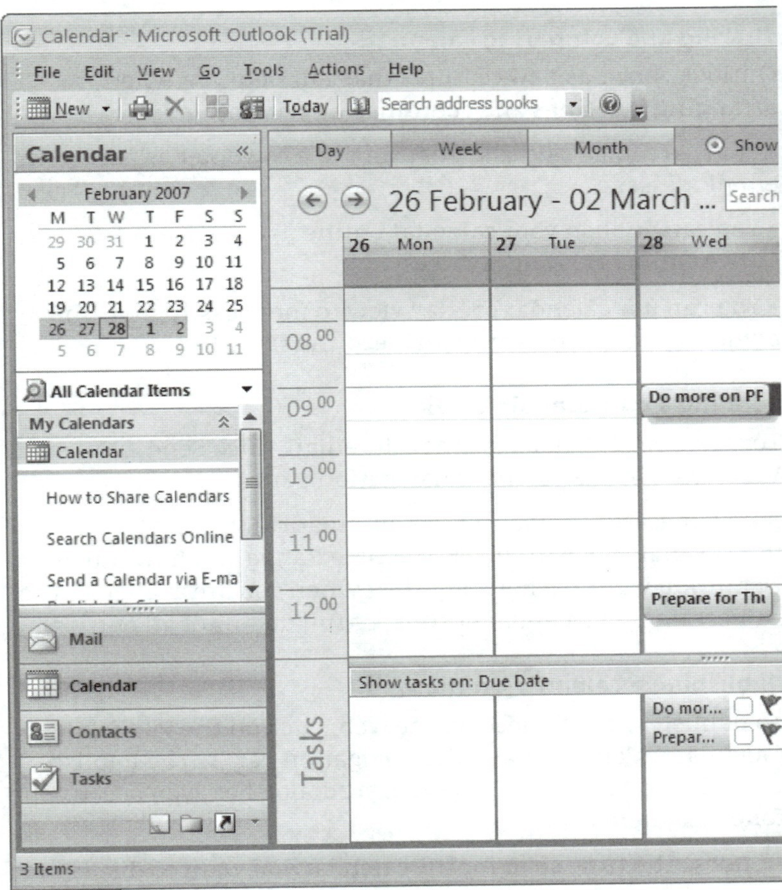

Tasks remain active on your To-Do Bar and also in your Task list and Calendar until you mark them as completed. If you don't manage to complete a task on your Daily Task List, it is automatically carried over to the next day.

Applying colour labels to tasks, appointments, messages and contacts

You can apply a colour category to any item you create in Outlook 2007 so that it stands out visually no matter which view you are using. For example, if you want an appointment you just created to be easy to spot on your Calendar, you can assign a colour to it using the Categorize control in the user interface. When the Appointment window is open, click the Categorize button and choose the colour you want from the displayed list.

Sharing and comparing calendars

Outlook 2007 has new features that can help you when arranging meetings and coordinating with others:

- You can send a calendar snapshot to a coworker as part of an email message
- You can publish your calendar online using Microsoft® Office Online Hosting Services
- You can use calendar overlay view to more easily spot when owners of calendars are available at the same time

Sending a calendar via email

To send your calendar to others by email, click Send A Calendar Via E-Mail in the Calendar navigation pane.

A new message window opens automatically, and you can use the dialog box to choose the Date Range and how much Detail you want to show (e.g. just when you are available, the subject lines of calendar entries, or full details of all entries).

Publishing a calendar on the web

To publish your calendar on the web, click on the Publish My Calendar link in the Calendar navigation bar. In the Publish Calendar To Microsoft Office Online dialog box, you specify the following items:

- Choose the time span for the calendar you want to display
- Select the level of detail to show (Availability only, Limited details, or Full details)
- Set permissions to determine who has access to your calendar
- Choose whether the calendar will be uploaded only once or

automatically as updated

After you publish the calendar online, you are given the option of sharing it with others. After you enter the email addresses of others you want to receive your calendar information, the web address of your calendar is sent, along with instructions on how others can access it.

Tip: Microsoft Office Online has a number of calendars you can download. Click Browse Calendars Online to look for calendar templates.

Taking control of the Inbox

Outlook 2007 includes a number of new features that can save you time and effort from setting up email accounts to filtering junk mail.

Find what you need faster

A new search box is available in all views (Mail, Calendar, Contacts, and Tasks). Just type the word or phrase you want to find.

Attachment Previews

The new ability to preview attachments saves you opening them in their parent applications (Word 2007, Excel 2007, etc.) just to view them. To preview an attachment, click the attachment, and the file displays in the body of the email message.

If the sender is not on your Safe Senders list, you might see a message before the preview appears, warning you of a potential security risk. If you trust the sender, click Preview File to continue the process.

Making emails Action Items

You can use the enhanced flagging feature to identify an important message as one you need to act on immediately. When you add the flag, the item is automatically added to the To-Do Bar.

Flagging Action Items for others

When other Outlook 2007 users receive a message you have flagged, it is added to their To-Do Bars as a task with a specific response date.

Setting up new email accounts

A new automated account setup feature asks for your email account name and password, and then does the rest.

Getting RSS news feeds

RSS is a great way of being notified of new content on any websites you choose, as long as they have RSS. You can receive RSS news feeds directly in your Outlook 2007 Inbox.

To use the RSS feature in Office Outlook 2007, double-click the RSS Feeds folder in your Personal Folders in the Mail navigation pane. A window appears telling you how to get started.

Improved junk mail filter

Office Outlook 2007 includes an enhanced Junk E-Mail Filter that catches incoming messages that could be junk mail — or its more dangerous counterpart, a phishing message — and then intercepts and eliminates it for you. When a message arrives that Office Outlook 2007 suspects might be a phishing message, a notification alerts you, and images and links in the message are disabled until you approve them.

When a message arrives that the filter thinks is spam, it puts it in the Junk folder. You should check this folder from time to time to see if there are any false positives, i.e. genuine messages falsely identified as junk.

You should identify such messages as not being spam by clicking on them and then choosing, Actions, Junk E-mail, Mark as Not Junk, or press Ctrl+Alt+J after selecting the message.

Blocking a sender

If you decide you don't want to see mail from a particular sender and would like it to be put in the Junk folder as soon as it arrives, you can add the sender to a list of blocked senders.

There are a number of ways to do this, but the easiest way to block an individual sender is to click a message from that sender, choose Actions, Junk E-mail and then click on Add Sender to Blocked Senders.

Adding people to the Safe Senders list

You can add the email addresses of people you trust to the Safe Senders list to make sure that messages they send you are never inadvertently filtered off as junk.

The easiest way to do this is to click on a message the person has already sent you, choose Actions, Junk E-mail and then click on either of these commands:

- Add Sender to Safe Senders List
- Add Sender's Domain (@example.com) to Safe Senders List

You'd choose the second if you trusted everyone using a particular company's or organization's domain, but you should not do it for any domain that spammers might use.

Postmarking

A new feature in Office Outlook 2007 automatically adds postmarks to messages you send. The postmark includes the list of recipients and the time you sent the message, which is what makes the postmark valid as an identification of that unique message. Spammers send thousands of emails out at one time from the same computer, which makes a unique postmark impossible. This makes it possible for the email program of the person receiving the postmarked email to be sure the message really is from you and so is not likely to be spam.

Creating email signatures

Email signatures are optional, but can be helpful to recipients. They are added to the end of a message, and usually tell people a little more about the sender, and can include full name, company name, postal address, web address, phone numbers, etc.

You might have different signatures for different types of email, depending on the information you wanted to share or the impression you wanted to convey.

You can create or edit a signature by going to Tools, Options and clicking the Mail Format tab, and then choosing Signatures. Click New to display the New Signature dialog box, type a descriptive name for your new signature, and click OK. You can then type the signature in the Edit area and click Save (and then OK) when done:

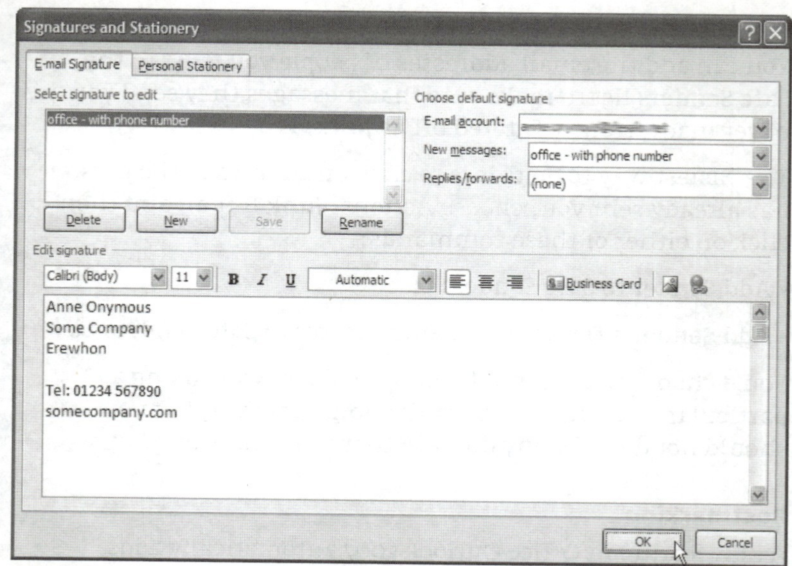

Creating electronic business cards

To share your contact information with others as an Electronic Business Card, first create your card. In the New Contact window, click Business Card in the Write tab to customize the default card that is created for a new contact. You can add photos and other special design elements.

To send electronic business cards to others via email or attach your business card to your outgoing messages, choose Options from the Tools menu and click the Mail Format tab in the Options dialog box. Click Signatures to display the Signatures and Stationery dialog box, then click Business Card in the Edit Signature area to display the Insert Business Card dialog box so that you can select the card you want to attach.

Creating new mail messages

Click on New or press Ctrl+N. Edit your message, check that the To and Subject fields are filled in and then click Send. If you want to Save the message before sending, perhaps so that you can work on it again later, click on Save or press Ctrl+S. If you close a message you've saved, you can find it in your draft folder.

When done editing, click Send.

Replying

To reply to a message, select or open the message and click on Reply (or press Ctrl+R).

Forwarding

To forward a message, select or open the message and click on Forward (or press Ctrl+F).

Attaching a file

To Attach a file to a message you are editing, click on Attach in the Include group, under the Message tab in the New Message window.

Then browse for the file, select it and click on Insert.

Sending to multiple recipients

To send mail to multiple recipients, type their addresses (or add them from your Contacts) in the To, Cc or Bcc fields in the New Message window, with each address separated by a comma. The Cc field is for sending copies, and people in the To field see who the copies are sent to. Any addresses in the Bcc field stay hidden from everyone.

Creating distribution lists

When you regularly send messages to the same group of people, it's easier to create a distribution list with all their addresses to save you the bother of entering them all every time you send a message. To do this, choose Actions, New Distribution List or press Ctrl+Shift+L.

In the form that pops up, type a name for the list, add people's addresses (either by hand or from your Contacts) and then click Save & Close.

To send a message to all the recipients in the list, type the list's name in the To field of a new message.

Keyboard shortcuts

Ctrl+N	Creates a new message when working in Mail, a new appointment when working in Calendar, a new contact when working in Contacts and a new Task when working in Tasks
Ctrl+R	Reply
Ctrl+F	Forward
Ctrl+S	Save a message, appointment, etc you are currently editing
Ctrl+P	Print
Ctrl+J	Marks a selected message that's not currently in the Junk folder as junk
Ctrl+Alt+J	Marks a selected message in the Junk folder as not being junk
Ctrl+Shift+L	Create a distribution list

4 • Microsoft® Office PowerPoint® 2007

PowerPoint 2007's new window

The command tabs in the new Fluent interface correspond to the main things you do when you create a presentation:

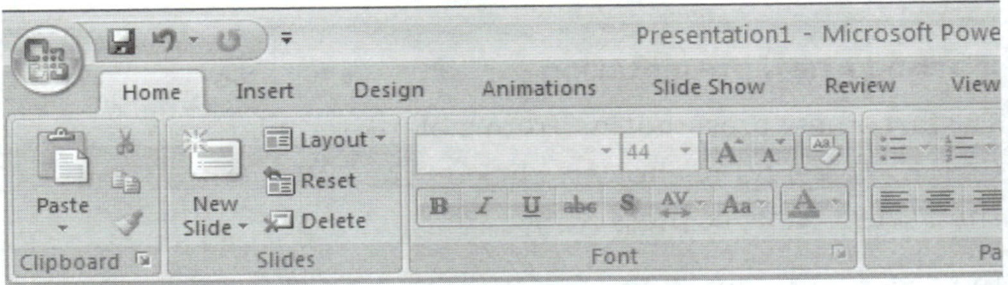

• ***The Home tab*** contains commands you are likely to use when you are creating and working with slides. You'll find commands for adding and deleting slides, choosing slide layouts, making font and paragraph choices, adding WordArt, and finding and replacing text.

• ***The Insert tab*** lets you add tables, pictures, diagrams, charts, Office shapes, links, text objects, and media clips.

• ***The Design tab*** has commands to set the page orientation, choose a presentation theme, design the slide background, and arrange objects on the slide.

• ***The Animations tab*** lets you choose animations and add sound, transitions, and timing selections.

• ***The Slide Show tab*** has commands for setting up, rehearsing, and displaying a slide show. It also has commands for recording narration, setting up dual monitors and changing display resolution.

• ***The Review tab*** offers the spelling checker and thesaurus, and provides translation and research tools. You'll also find commands for working with comments.

• ***The View tab*** provides a number of different options for the way in which you view your presentation. Choose among the traditional PowerPoint views, add gridlines and the ruler, make colour and grayscale changes, and work with presentation windows.

Tip: The Zoom slider in the bottom-right corner of the window is a helpful tool when you want to zoom in or out on a specific item in your presentation. In Normal view, use the Fit Slide To Current Window tool, to the right of the Zoom slider, to maximize the current slide within the size of the display window.

Starting a new presentation

To start a new presentation from a blank template, press Ctrl+N. To get more choices, click on the Office button and then select New, or press N.

In the New Presentation window that then opens you can:

• Browse through collections of templates by choosing from the template categories in the panel on the left side of the window

• Create a new presentation from scratch by clicking Blank Presentation

• Choose one of your own customized templates by clicking My Templates

• Build a new presentation based on one you already have by clicking New From Existing

• Get tips, ideas, and additional presentation templates from Microsoft Office Online

You can create your presentation by adding text and/or other elements to your slide and by creating new slides.

You can create new slides by clicking on the New Slide command in the Slides group of the Home tab, or by using the Outline mode in the navigation pane down the left-hand side of the PowerPoint window.

Clicking the down arrow of the New Slide command opens a gallery of Office Themes to choose from.

Using Outline mode will be familiar to anyone who has used earlier versions of PowerPoint:

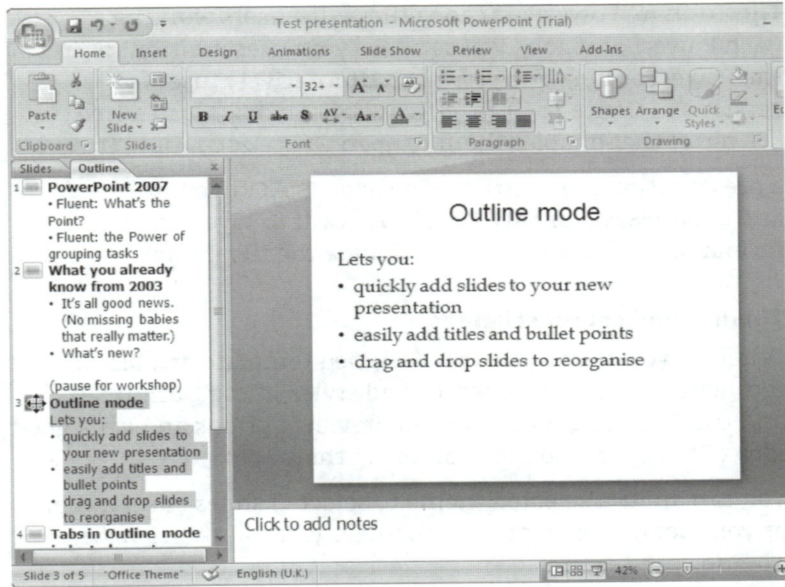

When working in Outline mode, typing a title for a slide and then pressing Enter will create a new slide. This makes it easy to quickly create all your slides with appropriate titles. You can also use Outline mode to include text content within slides without having to type anything in the main pane — just stay in the outline and use the Enter and Tab keys to organize slides and add basic content to them.

The Tab key indents (or 'demotes') elements in Outline mode (as does Alt+Shift+Right Arrow). Indented elements will appear, by default, as bullet points within the slides in the outline that are their 'parents' (you can easily remove or restyle bullets within individual slides using the Bullets command in the Paragraph group under the Home tab). To 'promote' any paragraph or point in your outline, use Shift+Tab (or Alt+Shift+Left Arrow). A promoted bullet point will move up in the hierarchy it's in, i.e. if it's already a main bullet point it will become a slide in its own right, with any associated sub-points becoming main points on that slide.

You can change the order of slides by dragging and dropping them, whether in Slides or Outline mode, or use Alt+Shift+Up Arrow or Alt+Shift+Down Arrow to move selected slides up or down.

Tip: To share PowerPoint 2007 files with users working with PowerPoint 2003 you can save your presentation in the PowerPoint 97–2003 format. Alternatively, users of versions of Office prior to Office 2007 can download a free file converter that enables them to open Office 2007 files. To save a presentation press Ctrl+S or click on the Office Button and choose Save (or Save As, if you want to save in a different format or location, or want to change the file name).

Themes and colour schemes

Whether you start with a predesigned template or a blank template, you can use themes and styles in the Design tab, and the Themes gallery lets you preview options and get a good idea of their effect before you select them.

You can apply a selected theme to selected slides or set a theme as your default presentation theme if you right-click on a Theme:

- in the Themes command set (under the Design tab), or
- in the Theme gallery that opens when you click on the More button in the Themes command set

You can easily modify themes and save them to the Themes gallery for later reuse, which is helpful if you have specific corporate colours that you'd like to use in your business presentations. To do this, first modify the slide and then click the Save Current Theme command at the bottom of the Themes gallery.

Choosing a New Colour Scheme

When you select a colour theme in PowerPoint 2007, the selection changes the background, all tables, text, and objects to match a consistent, coordinated, and cohesive set of colours.

The Colors command is in the Themes command set in the Design tab. Click the Colors down arrow to display the gallery of choices. Point to a new colour selection to get a preview of how it will affect the current presentation, and click to apply it.

Background Styles and Slide Master Layouts

The Background Styles command, in the Background group

under the Design tab, provides a collection of background styles you can apply to the current slide or to all slides in your presentation.

You can make additional choices for the background of your slides by clicking the Format Background command in the Background Styles gallery.

The Format Background dialog box that appears enables you to choose a picture or texture for the background, change colours and gradients for fills, etc:

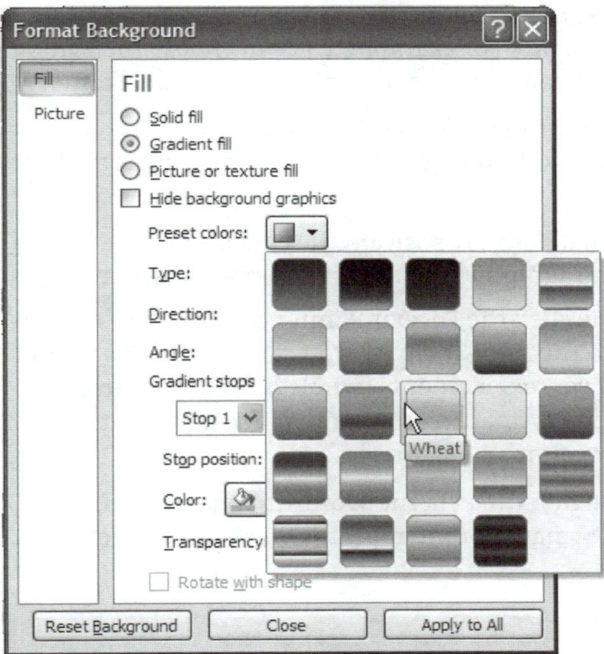

Custom Slide Master Layouts

In PowerPoint 2007, you can create custom slide master layouts. You can put placeholders (elements in position ready to be filled with media objects, text, etc) on your custom slide master layout using Insert Placeholder in the Master Layout command tab of the Slide Master tab.

The Slide Master tab and the Insert Placeholder command become available when you select the SlideMaster command in the View tab.

Formatting text

Formatting text in PowerPoint is very similar to formatting text in Word in that the Home tab has font and paragraph command sets, and the Mini Toolbar becomes available whenever text is selected or whenever you right-click on text:

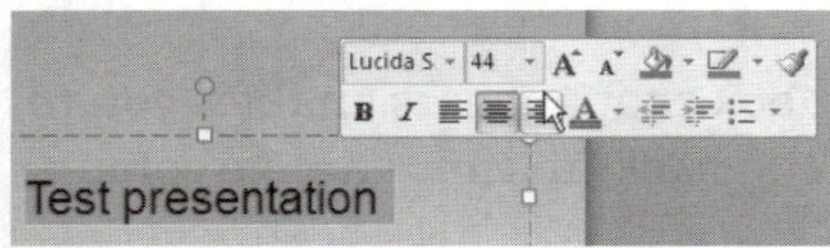

In addition, text can be formatted via the Themes group under the Design tab. For example, you can choose the Fonts command to preview changes in a gallery of available fonts.

Tip: The Format Painter is a useful tool for copying the formatting already applied to any text and applying it to other bits of text.

To use the Format Painter, position the cursor within the word, line or paragraph using the format you'd like to copy and then double click the Format Painter command in the Home tab (or in the Mini Toolbar). You can then click on other words or drag over text elements (whole lines or paragraphs) to apply the same formatting to them. When done, click the Format Painter command again.

Text can also be modified via the WordArt Styles command set under the Format tab that appears whenever we click on or select text:

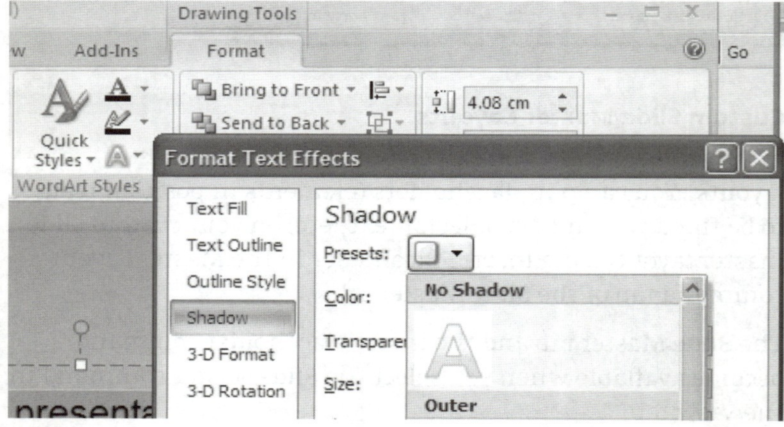

Shapes

Shapes are available from either the Drawing group under the Home tab, or the Illustrations group of the Insert tab (or from the Insert Shapes group of the Format tab, when available):

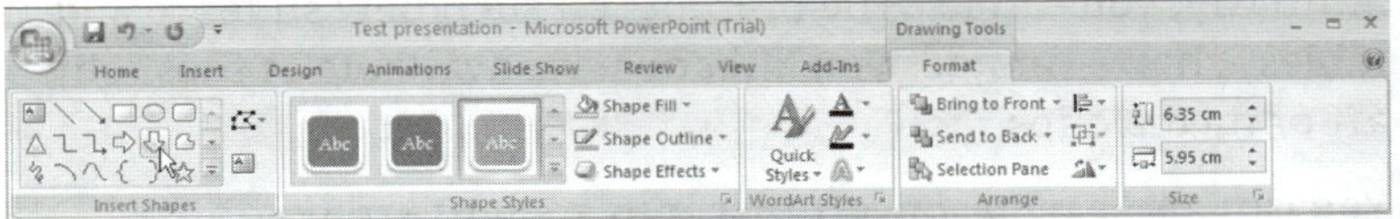

When you click on the Shapes command, a gallery appears for you to choose a shape from.

Once you've added a shape to your slide (or whenever such an object is selected), the Format tab appears, with a number of tools that enable you to work with the selected shape:

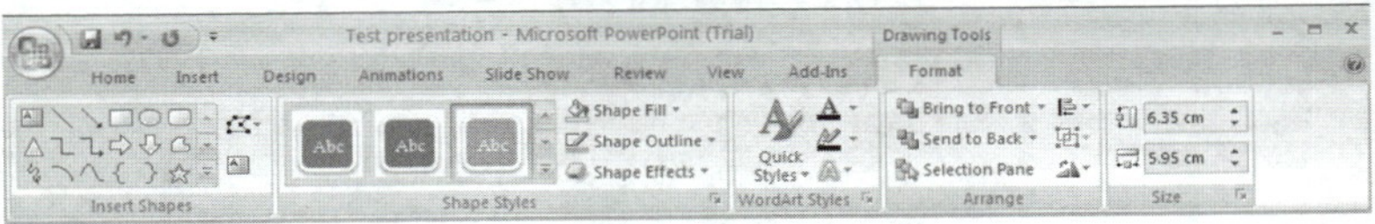

The Quick Styles command enables you to choose the lighting, colour, style, and shadow of the shape and you can use WordArt Quick Styles to control the look of any text you add to the shape. The Arrange and Size command sets give you options for the size and position of the object.

You can click on and drag the handles on a shape's placeholder (the small circles, squares and diamonds on the outline that surrounds it when it's selected) to rotate, stretch or resize it.

Diagram Tools

The SmartArt diagramming tool enables you to create flexible, customizable diagrams:

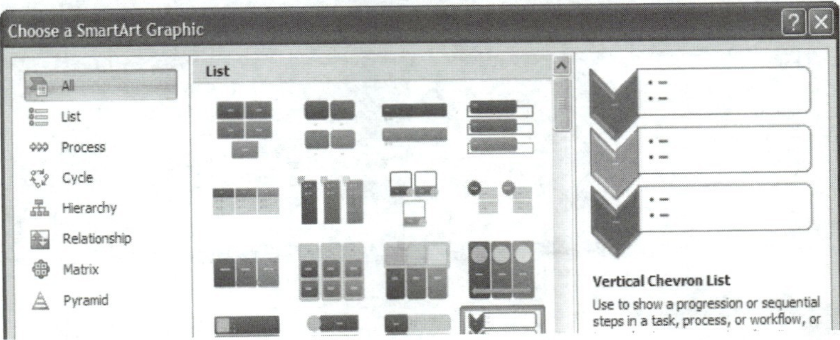

You can add diagrams to your slides by clicking the Insert tab and choosing SmartArt, or by clicking on the Insert SmartArt Graphic prompt on any new slide that has prompts for content.

Similarly, you can use the prompts on such new slides to add tables, charts, images you already have available as files, clip art or media clips.

You can also easily convert text into a SmartArt diagram. Right-click the content area of a slide that has relevant text in it, hover over Convert to SmartArt and then select the diagram type of your choice:

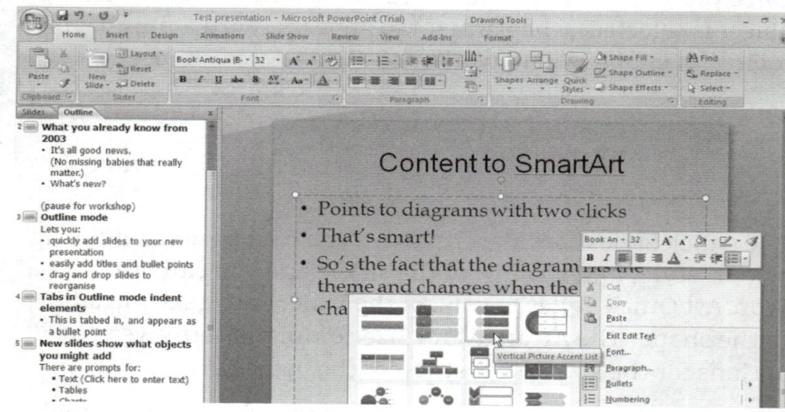

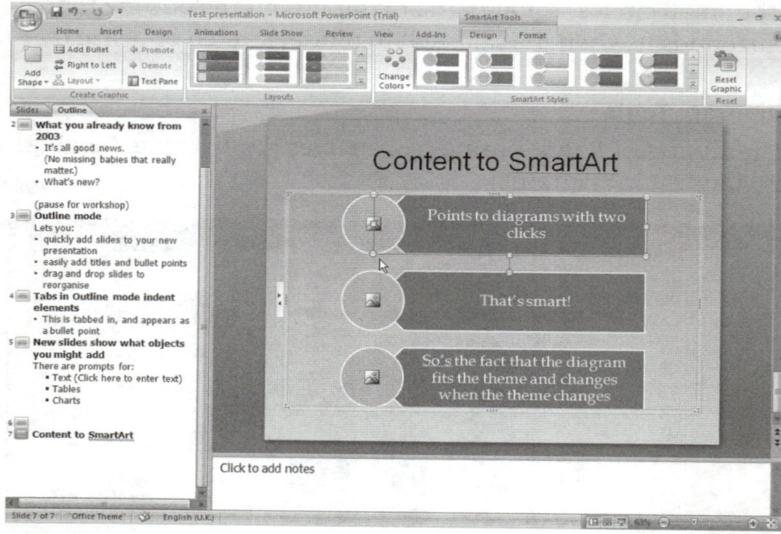

Transitions

Slide transitions are used to create a short pause between slides that helps maintain the audience's interest and helps you control the pace of your presentation. Beware of employing too much variety in transition effects within a single presentation, however. The use of different types of transition can be distracting to your audience, who may go away remembering more about your transitions than your message. It may be tempting to pick a handful or more transitions from the nearly 60 offered by PowerPoint 2007, but it's much better to use just one or two transition effects so that audiences are not distracted from you, your presentation and your message.

To create transitions, select a slide and click on the Animation tab, if it isn't already active. In the Transition to This Slide command set, click on the transitions already displayed in the Transition Scheme command, or click on its More button to display the gallery. Let the mouse pointer hover over an option to preview its effect and click to apply:

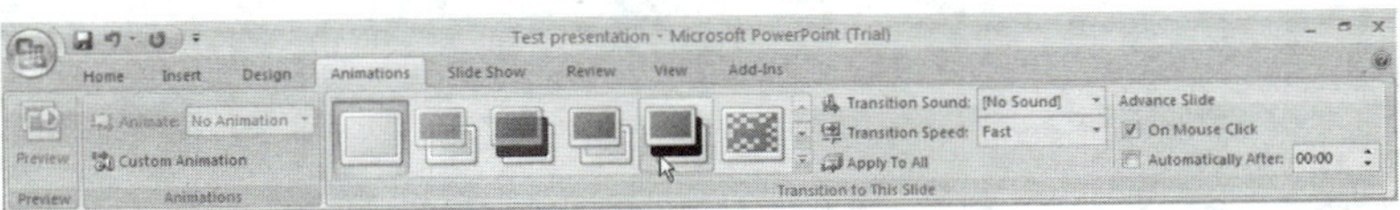

You can choose a sound effect from the same command set, as well as the speed.

If you'd like to apply the same transition to the whole presentation, click on the Apply to All command. When transitions are applied to a slide, a star appears on it in the navigation pane (in Slides mode, not Outline Mode) so you can easily see if any slides are missing a transition. Finally, set whether you want the trigger for moving from one slide to the next to be a mouse click or a set period of time:

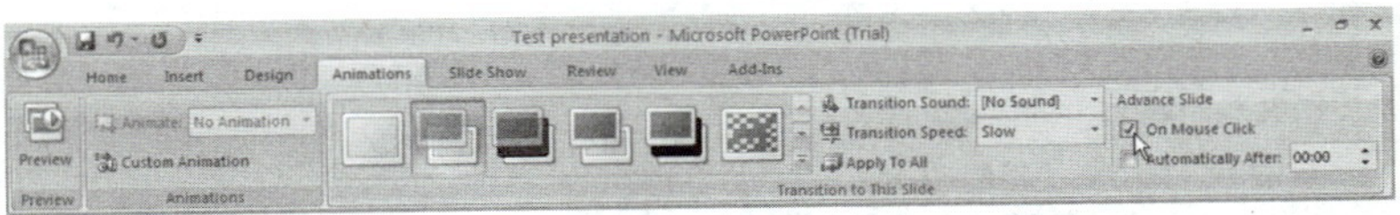

Animations

Animations should enhance your content, rather than distract from its message. It's also important to match animations to your audience. For a young, creative audience, greater use of animation may be more appropriate than for a formal presentation to a board, for example.

A popular use of animation is to make bullet points appear one at a time, controlled by a click from the presenter. This is an effective strategy because it:

- Gives you control of the display of items in your presentation
- Prevents the audience from being distracted by points you're not talking about
- Enables you to hide surprise points until you are ready to reveal them
- Allows you to put emphasis on individual bullets

To create individual bullet animations, choose a slide with the bullets you'd like to animate and click the placeholder that contains them. In the Animations command set (under the Animation tab) click on the Custom Animation command:

The Custom Animation pane will display. Next, click Add Effect and choose the effect you'd like to apply.

The effect is initially applied to all bullets. Click the expand contents button and click the first bullet. To make it appear only when you click the mouse, click on the Change button and select Entrance, and then click the effect you want (again, possibly, if it's the same effect you chose earlier for all bullets). Next select the On Click option in the Start list for that button:

This will delay its appearance until you click with the mouse during the presentation.

Set the effects you want for the button in the Direction and Speed lists, also:

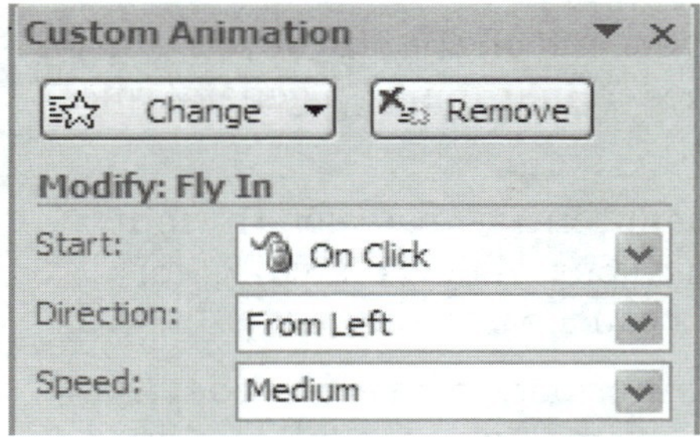

Do the same for the other bullets, making sure they are numbered in the Start list in the order in which you would like them to appear. To preview the effect, click the Slide Show tab and then the From Current Slide command in the Start Slide Show command set:

To leave the slide show and return to the PowerPoint window, press the Escape key.

Tips for PowerPoint presentations

The slides

- Match your presentation to your audience (see Animations, for example).
- Try to reflect any company colour scheme or style in your presentation.
- Try to make slides consistent. Avoid using multiple typefaces and colours. Ensure that elements on every slide (such as the company logo) are always in the same place, so as not to distract your audience from the content. At the same time, try not to use the same layout on every slide, as this may become monotonous. So, for example, the first slide might be title only, the next, title and text, the following one, text and graphics, then diagram or table, etc only, and so on.

- Resist the temptation to use fancy fonts. They can be difficult to read, especially from a distance.
- The font size you use will depend on the size of your screen and your audience's distance from it, but as a general rule, go for at least 20 point size.
- Make sure there is sufficient contrast between the font colour and the background colour. Yellow on white, for example, is nearly always a bad idea.
- Do not include too much information on each slide. As a general rule, 1–5 items is optimal (where a bullet point counts as one item).

You

- Try not to feel tied to a screen, or use a desk or lectern as a safety barrier. Move about freely and engage your audience.
- Ensure you make eye contact with every part of your audience and, if appropriate, encourage them to answer questions and offer opinions during the presentation, rather that just at the end.
- Remember that you and your message are the main focus. The slides are there to support you.
- Practise your talk beforehand, and if possible video yourself. Reviewing the video will help immensely to improve your technique; refined technique and well-rehearsed presentations help to build your confidence.